THE
MORE OR LESS
DEFINITIVE
GUIDE
TO
SELF-CARE

ANNA BORGES

Illustrations by Bob Scott

THE EXPERIMENT
NEW YORK

The Experiment, LLC
220 East 23rd Street, Suite 600
New York, NY 10010-4658
theexperimentpublishing.com

This book contains the opinions and ideas of its author. It is intended to provide helpful and informative material on the subjects addressed in the book. It is sold with the understanding that the author and publisher are not engaged in rendering medical, health, or any other kind of personal professional services in the book. The author and publisher specifically disclaim all responsibility for any liability, loss, or risk—personal or otherwise—that is incurred as a consequence, directly or indirectly, of the use and application of any of the contents of this book.

THE EXPERIMENT and its colophon are registered trademarks of The Experiment, LLC. Many of the designations used by manufacturers and sellers to distinguish their products are claimed as trademarks. Where those designations appear in this book and The Experiment was aware of a trademark claim, the designations have been capitalized.

The Experiment's books are available at special discounts when purchased in bulk for premiums and sales promotions as well as for fund-raising or educational use. For details, contact us at info@theexperimentpublishing.com.

Library of Congress Cataloging-in-Publication Data

Names: Borges, Anna, author.
Title: The more or less definitive guide to self-care / Anna Borges.
Description: New York : The Experiment, 2019.
Identifiers: LCCN 2019024873 (print) | LCCN 2019024874 (ebook) | ISBN
    9781615196104 | ISBN 9781615196111 (ebook)
Subjects: LCSH: Self-care, Health. | Well-being. | Mental health. |
    Spiritual life.
Classification: LCC RA776.95 .B67 2019 (print) | LCC RA776.95 (ebook) |
    DDC 613--dc23
LC record available at https://lccn.loc.gov/2019024873
LC ebook record available at https://lccn.loc.gov/2019024874

ISBN 978-1-61519-610-4
Ebook ISBN 978-1-61519-611-1

Cover and text design by Beth Bugler
Author photograph by Kim Hoyos

Manufactured in China

First printing November 2019
10 9 8 7 6 5 4 3 2

CONTENTS

INTRODUCTION

What Is Self-Care?

The concept of self-care is deceptively simple: making time to take care of yourself for the benefit of your overall mental and physical well-being. But if you're a human who exists in this world—the *real* world, where burnout, depression, anxiety, pain, illness, trauma, oppression, shitty families, violence, tragedy, breakups, divorces, death, unemployment, addiction, and good ol'-fashioned bad times exist—you know that "taking care of yourself" is never a simple thing.

Because of that, when creating a guide to self-care, I didn't want to try to reinvent the wheel—it's such a personal, complicated, sprawling thing that it would be disingenuous, not to mention unhelpful, to try to create a straightforward how-to guide. For some people, self-care is doing the bare minimum to make it through the day; for others it's all about indulging and pampering and de-stressing. For most of us, it's a wide spectrum of decisions and actions that soothe and fortify us against all the shit we deal with in the world. There are just too many ways to practice self-care out there to sit here and tell anyone definitively how to do it.

But before we get into that, let's talk history first.

Believe it or not, self-care originally caught on as a medical concept. Doctors knew that health-related care couldn't revolve around appointments, hospitalizations, and the constant guidance of health professionals. Not only is it hard to get people to keep up on their checkups and appointments (who else is guilty of putting off going to the doctor as long as possible?), but defining health care only as what requires professional intervention ignores something really important: that taking care of ourselves has to be an ongoing daily commitment.

Doctors have always been invested in the ways we can manage our own health through "self-care"—broadly defined as the personal effort we put into staying well, preventing disease, managing our minor ailments, and maintaining control over our chronic diseases and conditions.

Later, academics applied the concept to people who worked in "helping professions" such as therapists, EMTs, and social workers, and in other stressful and draining occupations. These people especially needed to learn ways to protect their emotional and physical well-being because the demands of their work—sitting with people in their pain and struggles— had the capacity to take a huge toll on their health.

Self-care became political with the rise of the women's movement and the civil rights movement. For women and especially people of color, taking their health into their own hands through self-care was an act of claiming autonomy over their bodies in the face of a white, patriarchal medical system that was failing them. Self-described "black, lesbian, mother, warrior, poet" Audre Lorde wrote, "Caring for myself is not self-indulgence, it is self-preservation, and that is an act of political warfare." And while these words referenced her battle with liver cancer in *A Burst of Light*, they are also often recognized as one of the roots of our modern understanding of self-care as a radical act.

CARING FOR
MYSELF IS NOT
SELF-INDULGENCE,
IT IS SELF-
PRESERVATION,
AND THAT IS AN
ACT OF POLITICAL
WARFARE.
—AUDRE LORDE

Since then, the concept of self-care has exploded kaleidoscopically. By now, much has been written about self-care: what it is, what it isn't, what it can do, what it can't. It has been bastardized, commercialized, reclaimed, redefined. But no matter what it means for you personally, self-care should also be a lifestyle—a highly personalizable lifestyle—because taking care of yourself and taking ownership of your health isn't something you do just once. It's a responsibility we have to ourselves.

Luckily, as responsibilities go, it can be a pretty enjoyable one.

What Does "Self-Care Is a Lifestyle" Really Mean, Though?

Don't worry, committing to the lifestyle of taking care of yourself doesn't mean that it's something that you have to do 24-7. Not everything in your life can be self-care—we'd never get anything done—but self-care *can* permeate most of the corners of your life. Along those lines, self-care usually falls into at least one of these four categories:

1. NOURISHING YOUR BODY

The things you do to take care of your physical self, such as moving, drinking enough water, taking care of hygiene, and keeping up on your medical appointments. You probably notice you feel better or worse depending on your overall health habits and how you treat your body. That's because mental and physical health are so closely intertwined; sleeping patterns, diet, exercise, caffeine, alcohol, medication, hormonal shifts, daylight, relaxation, and recovery can cause changes in your moods, thought patterns, and overall emotional well-being.

2. NOURISHING YOUR MIND

The things that promote positive emotional and mental health, such as developing coping mechanisms, cultivating self-awareness, correcting negative thought patterns, and accepting your vulnerability. A lot of these practices can come from the help of a professional—such as a counselor or therapist—but it requires work on your part, too. Going to the therapist isn't like going to the doctor for an infection where you leave with medicine and can expect to be better in a week or two. You have to build an arsenal of fortifying habits to have at your disposal when things get rough.

3. NOURISHING YOUR RELATIONSHIPS

The care and keeping of support systems in your life. No matter how introverted or independent we are, we all need social connection. Loneliness is largely considered a growing epidemic, and the impact it can have on your health is no joke. Chronic loneliness can increase depression and anxiety, and some studies even point toward it contributing to early death. So yes, we need our people, we need to get out into the world, and we need to feel *part of*. On top of that, social self-care involves learning to set boundaries and knowing how to distinguish between healthy and unhealthy bonds.

4. NOURISHING YOUR SPIRIT

The intangible ways you feed your soul and create meaning in the world. There's no one way or reason to be a spiritual person. It could be about bringing creativity, curiosity, and wisdom into your life. It could be about strengthening your relationship with yourself or the world around you. It could be about finding some higher guiding path or power to make existing a little easier or more meaningful. Whether that's practicing religion or magic, doing rituals, meditating, learning astrology, setting intentions, or whatever speaks to you, spirituality gives you a way to tap into something beyond yourself.

Of course, not everything you do will fall perfectly under one of these umbrellas—it's more about viewing self-care as a holistic practice than sorting everything into neat little boxes.

What Self-Care Isn't

Just as there are a million and one possible definitions of self-care, there are also a lot of ways it can be misinterpreted and misused. Here are a few things to keep in mind to make sure you're not squandering the potential benefits of self-care:

1. SELF-CARE ISN'T SELFISH.

There's a frustrating misconception that anything that is not 100 percent self*less* is self*ish*. But taking care of ourselves and caring for and considering others are not mutually exclusive. In fact, taking care of our own health and well-being empowers us to be better friends, partners, coworkers, bosses, family members, and humans. Without doing the essential work of showing up for ourselves, how can we expect to be in any shape to show up for others? As the old saying goes, you have to put your oxygen mask on before you can assist anyone else.

All that said, though, taking care of yourself is a reason in and of itself. You don't need to justify your self-care efforts by enumerating the ways it benefits everyone besides you. You deserve care for its own sake.

2. SELF-CARE ISN'T AN EXCUSE.

OK, I know we just established that self-care is not inherently selfish but, like anything, it can be exploited. Somewhere along the line, the language of self-care grew past concepts like "learn self-compassion" and "remember to bathe" to include "make yourself feel good by any means necessary, even at the expense of other people." Which, *no*.

When we say self-care isn't selfish, we mean that our needs are important and worth attention. But that doesn't mean that we're not capable of using self-care as an instrument of selfishness. I'm sure you've seen people slap ~self-care~ on just about anything as a justification for bad or irresponsible behavior. Hell, I'm sure you've done it yourself. I know I've been guilty of it, for sure. Cancel your plans: self-care! Blow off obligations in favor of a facemask and a glass of wine: self-care! Spend money you don't really have: self-care!

So, as you go about attending to your needs, respect those around you and be honest with yourself about your motivations, your impact on others, and whether you're just hiding an excuse to do whatever you want behind a smoke screen of self-care.

3. SELF-CARE ISN'T SELF-RELIANCE.

One of the most common criticisms of self-care is that it's unfair and unrealistic to put all this pressure on yourself to be in charge of your own well-being. And that's absolutely true—there's nothing more annoying than the old adage that you can "choose happiness," as if you've always had the power to zap away your misery and have just been squandering it.

None of us has the capacity to soothe all that ails us on our own. Self-care is as much about opening yourself up to the many ways others can help you as it is about taking care of yourself. It's educating yourself on resources, giving yourself permission to access professional help without shame, and asking for what you need.

4. SELF-CARE ISN'T ONE-SIZE-FITS-ALL.

Not only is the self-care that works for you going to be completely different from what works for someone else, but the appropriate form of self-care for *you* will look different from day to day. The self-care you need when you're anxious is going to look different from the self-care you need when you're lonely. And what makes you feel better when you're a little sad might be impossible to do when you're incredibly depressed. And hey, maybe no matter what, you are never going to be a person who meditates. (Same here.)

All that said, it's not always easy to tell what you need. You can only find out through experimentation and by listening to what your body tells you—and then honoring those findings.

5. SELF-CARE ISN'T A CURE.

The goal of self-care is an ever-morphing target, so concentrate on getting to know yourself and your needs instead of thinking in terms of cures and fixes, solutions and antidotes. Meditation isn't going to cure your anxiety. Setting boundaries doesn't guarantee people will respect them. Drinking water isn't going to transform you into a dewy health goddess. Getting out into nature won't wipe away the problems that you left behind inside.

All we have is the ability to try our best—whatever that means, each day, because it *will* change—and decide that, OK, this self-care thing is worthy of my time because I am worthy of being taken care of.

A Note on Accessibility, Consumerism, and Privilege

We can't talk about self-care without talking about how—despite all its merits—it doesn't exist in a vacuum. Simply put, self-care isn't accessible or even close to a top priority for everyone. Not only has it become inexplicably linked with consumerism as brands capitalize on the movement and, in the name of self-care, push everything from boutique fitness classes to $80 crystal water bottles, but even when self-care is at its best, some people simply just . . . have more important things to deal with. Racism, ableism, queerphobia, transphobia, fatphobia, sexism, and classism all influence our ability or inability to practice self-care—especially when mainstream self-care is based on a very specific vision of what day-to-day life should look like and an assumption of certain privileges many people just don't have.

There are communities in which constant injustice and oppression, as well as ongoing and generational traumas, impact how individuals are able to take care of themselves.

There are people for whom self-care is a laughable idea when they're stretched thin tending to basic needs such as affording food and shelter for their families.

There are those with serious mental illnesses whom the mental health industry regularly fails: low-functioning individuals who make up a disproportionate share of homelessness, incarceration, and suicide. We often leave out those with psychotic, violent, or otherwise debilitating symptoms in our conversations about mental health because they're harder to package in an uplifting movement. What does self-care mean to someone pushed out of a psychiatric facility because there aren't enough beds?

Sweeping change is needed across the board: in mental health services, in our burnout culture, in affordable healthcare, in our discriminatory and oppressive society that leaves the most vulnerable populations most susceptible to poor mental health. Self-care has its purpose and can be life-changing for many, but in advocating for it, we can't forget that the onus to protect our mental health isn't only on self-care—it's on the system that makes practicing self-care necessary in the first place.

How to Use This Book

This book is full of tips, activities, exercises, and stories both from therapists and from people who have been there, including myself. I'm not a therapist, but as a health reporter, I am in constant dialogue with therapists, psychologists, and doctors and have hoarded the lessons they've taught me over the years like gold. Not to mention, I have been in a *lot* of therapy myself and have learned my own tricks through personal experience, too. The more techniques you learn, the more tools you have at your disposal to finesse your own personal self-care routine.

It's my hope that this book will help you gather skills and practices to put in your toolkit. I'm not here to tell you the right way to do self-care because, honestly, it has to be what you need it to be. The ideas you'll find here are meant to be a starting point—a kind of one-stop shop for your mind, body, and soul when you need it. They are big and little, preventive and curative, concrete and abstract. Not every idea will apply to you and your needs, but they will be here for you to draw on when you need inspiration.

Experiment with them—find out what works for you when you're angry, when you're sad, when you're lonely, when you're traumatized, when you're grieving, when you're numb, when you're stressed. Commit to prioritize caring for yourself and finding the things you can do every day that make you feel stronger.

And through all that, discover your own definition of self-care.

SELF-CARE

A *to* Z

A. A. Milne / Quotes are hit-or-miss for a lot of people and can be so personal, so you won't find a ton in this book. But one quote has always served as the foundation of my self-care: "Promise me you'll always remember: You're braver than you believe, and stronger than you seem, and smarter than you think."

I repeat this quote (originally from the movie *Pooh's Grand Adventure*, which was written by Karl Geurs and Carter Crocker, but that I'm filing under A. A. Milne, the well-known creator of Winnie-the-Pooh who wrote the book that inspired the quote) when I feel helpless in the face of my own illnesses, emotions, and circumstances. When I feel like I can't do anything, I remind myself that I have the capacity to be brave, to be strong, and to be smart.

In order to practice self-care, at least for me, you have to go into it with a little bit of optimism: a belief that you have it in you to self-soothe, to strengthen yourself, to be a little more OK. Only then does this, *any of this*, work.

ACCEPTS / Sometimes when you're feeling a strong emotion—anger, jealousy, sadness, etc.—you're not in a position to problem-solve it away. Feelings are loud! At that point, your immediate priority can simply be to ease the feelings so you're not just sitting in distress. ACCEPTS is an acronym representing a group of distraction skills that can help you tolerate and soothe a negative emotion until you're able to address the situation.

ACCEPTS comes from dialectical behavioral therapy (DBT), a type of mindfulness developed by Dr. Marsha Linehan that's focused on practical skills to regulate emotions and help you take responsibility for unhealthy or disruptive behavior. The goal is to access what Linehan calls your "wise mind"—which is an integration of your emotional mind and your reasonable mind, because our emotions can get in the way of reason, but reason can't magically overcome our emotions. You need to engage with both.

Dialectical behavioral therapy is typically used to help people with borderline personality disorder, chronic suicidal ideation, post-traumatic stress disorder, or eating disorders, but more and more therapists are integrating DBT techniques in their work with all sorts of mental health issues.

ACCEPTS STANDS FOR:

Activities: Turn to a hobby, play a video game, play a sport.

Contributing: Babysit for a friend so they can go out, volunteer.

Comparisons: Whether looking toward real-life examples or tragic movies, it might make you feel better to consider the ways your current situation isn't worse.

Emotions: Try to channel the opposite emotion of the one you're trying to manage. For example, if you're sad or angry, watch funny YouTube videos.

Push away: Visualize building a wall between you and the negative emotion, or imagine it as a solid mass that you can push away. Imagine the source of your anger growing smaller and smaller until it disappears.

Thoughts: Do something that requires your full cognitive attention. You don't need to do any critical thinking—strong emotions can obviously cloud that—but read a book, focusing on everything at a sentence level.

Sensation: Holding a cube of ice is one of the most popular distracting sensations, since it's sharp but not painful. But you can also play with more comforting sensations, like soft textures or warm water.

These suggestions may seem fairly straightforward to some people, but when you're in your emotional mind, it can be hard to access coping skills. Acronyms like ACCEPTS (and more to come) are shortcuts to your self-care toolbox.

Affirmations / ~Positive affirmations~ are prescribed as an
antidote to so many problems under the sun, such as low self-esteem,
lack of motivation, anxiety, guilt, and pretty much any negativity in
your life. The idea is, with enough repetition, positive thoughts and
beliefs will stick, changing the way you think and live your life.

Most of the time, though, affirmations are pretty useless—at
least if you're doing them the way they're most widely understood.
According to psychologist Dr. Guy Winch in his book *Emotional
First Aid*, if you don't really believe an affirmation, you're going to
make yourself feel even *worse*. Affirmations only work when they fall
within "the range of believability," otherwise your mind rejects them.
And over-the-top affirmations like *I am fierce, no one can make me feel
inferior* or *I'm a strong and capable person who can accomplish whatever I
put my mind to* might not fall within the range of believability if you're
someone who needs affirmations in the first place.

All that said, you might still be interested in positive affirmations,
and that's OK! There's reason to believe that affirmations effect
change because of the science of neuroplasticity—aka, the brain's
ability to rewire and reorganize itself by forming new neural
connections throughout life. So, if you want to give it a try, it's worth
coming up with affirmations that you believe but may just need to be
reminded of from time to time, or affirmations that remind you of
your values.

What those affirmations actually are will depend on you, but I can
say that I have a mug on my desk that reminds me YOU DID NOT WAKE
UP TODAY TO BE MEDIOCRE in big, bold letters, and whenever I see it,
I'm like, "You're right. I didn't." And I get back to work.

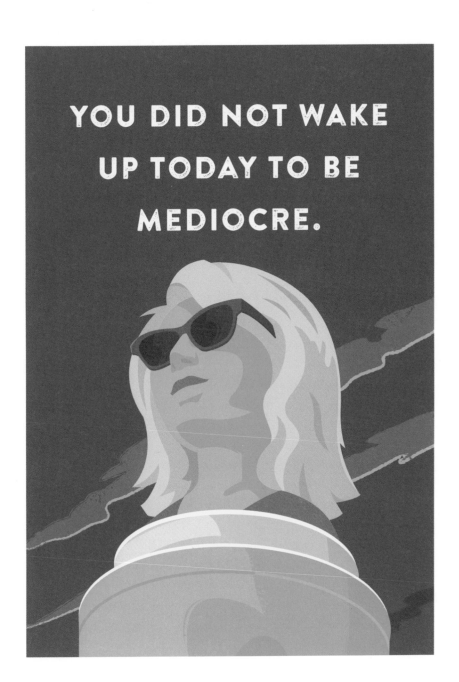

Alarms / No matter how long I'd been on the same antidepressants, birth control, and vitamin regimen, there was a time when I'd forget at least once a week to take my medley of pills. For a while, I didn't bother setting an alarm to remind myself. I had a weekly pillbox; I should have been able to remember to take it! Everything out there was telling me that if I did something long enough, it would eventually become a habit. Second nature. But it never did, and I kept missing doses and wondering why I felt like shit. So I set a daily alarm.

Maybe your alarm isn't for medication. Maybe it's for remembering to eat or hydrate or say something nice about yourself. There's no shame in utilizing tools for healthy habits.

Altars / Altars—structures where offerings are made for religious or spiritual purposes—are typically associated with shrines, temples, churches, and other sites of worship, but they've also found a place in modern homes as spaces of contemplation, ritual work, and healing. At their most basic, altars are spaces, big or small, to keep physical reminders of things that are important to you: memories, values, goals, intentions. Think: photos of loved ones, crystals with properties you want to draw on, quotes that empower you or make you think, meaningful trinkets or talismans, flowers or other reminders of nature, handwritten letters, or candles. They can take up whole shelves or exist on a cloth in a corner of your closet.

If you're someone who finds comfort in decorating your corkboard with photos and movie stubs, holding on to old mementos, or even curating a Pinterest board, chances are you'd feel a strong connection with an altar and find pleasure in the act of creating one.

Anticipation / Foresight is an incredibly useful tool when it

comes to taking care of yourself. When you're deep in feelings of hurt or frustration, proper self-care winds up being the furthest thing from your mind and you can wind up turning to less-than-helpful coping mechanisms. Obviously, you won't always be able to plan ahead, but take advantage of the times when you can—like when you're about to spend the holidays with your difficult family or are looking down the barrel of an important deadline. When you know that stressful, aggravating, or otherwise unsavory times are on the horizon, you can get ready for it. You can stock your fridge with ready-to-eat meals. You can minimize distractions, or get ready for them. You can prepare a whole emergency self-care contingency plan. Which, luckily for you, is something this whole book is going to get you ready to do.

Ask for Help / Because you can't and shouldn't do everything

alone, especially when you're struggling. I know, I know. Easier said than done. But you need to care for yourself enough to accept when you can't do it alone, and give the people around you the opportunity to prove they care about you, too. I mean, how many times do loved ones say, "Let me know if you need anything!" Chances are they really mean it, but sometimes you actually have to *let them know*. People won't always know the best way to help you.

So ask. Ask them to help you make a difficult phone call, clean up your room, go to the grocery store with you, *anything*.

If you're someone who always hesitates to "inconvenience" people, asking for help doesn't have to mean asking for work. It can just be about asking for support. Text a friend and ask them to tell you three ways you are powerful, or why they like you. Ask for a pep talk. Ask for a favorite memory.

Astrology /

Astrology / For the uninitiated who may only glance at your horoscope when you happen upon it or laugh at a meme describing "the signs as" when someone drops it into the group chat, you are more than what you probably know as your zodiac sign. That one, determined by your birthday, is your sun sign. In addition to that, you have a whole chart of signs, one for each planet, derived from the unique snapshot of what the planets looked like in the sky around your little head when you entered the world. To look up your chart, you need the day, year, time, and location of your birth.

And each of those planets represents a different part of you. Your sun sign represents your ego and your sense of self, whereas your moon sign governs your subconscious, your emotions, and who you are when no one is watching. Mercury is all about communication, while Venus sheds light on love and what we need in relationships. And on and on and on. You could fill a whole book on tips for decoding your birth chart, but I'll let you fall down that rabbit hole yourself, otherwise we might be here all day.

The important part, it turns out, is that you are basically a *galaxy* of a person, not just one cluster of stars. And what you can do with that information hidden in your chart can be both illuminating and healing. Astrology can be a permission slip to begin to accept who you

are and what you have to work with as you try to love, understand, forgive, and improve yourself.

You don't have to believe in this stuff in your heart of hearts for it to be a tool, either. In fact, approaching astrology with a healthy dose of skepticism is a solid way to flex your self-awareness muscles. You can dig through your chart, hold things up to the light, and decide what rings true and what doesn't, and what all of that tells you about yourself.

Throughout this book, there are a lot of hobby suggestions because hobbies *are* self-care. They provide you with a sense of accomplishment, teach you about yourself, introduce you to new people, concepts, and facts about the world, and give you something to do when you're in desperate need of a distraction.

Avoid / You probably know that, as a general rule, avoidance isn't awesome. But there's also something to be said for knowing what you have the bandwidth to weather at any given moment—especially when it comes to triggers, overwhelming or uncomfortable environments, or draining people. Throughout your life, there will be good reasons to face these challenges, preferably when you're equipped with the right tools (we'll get to that later), but there will be instances when it'll just do more harm than good.

Check in with yourself and think about whether some situation or task will exacerbate feelings of anxiety, depression, fear, lack of safety, or anger you're already dealing with. If your gut says yes, today might not be the day. *See also* Yes.

THE MORE YOU KNOW, THE SOONER YOU CAN FIND THE PROPER AVENUES FOR HELP AND HEALING—AND FEEL LESS ALONE.

Awareness / Mental health struggles are *so* pervasive nowadays, and yet only about half of people dealing with mental illness seek out treatment. A lot of the time, people think that whatever they're struggling with is just . . . kind of how things are for everyone. It took me until senior year of college to go to our campus counseling center because until then it hadn't occurred to me that I shouldn't be struggling to get out of bed in the morning. I thought, *It's college, everyone's kind of depressed! I just need to get my shit together and stop being so lazy!* And I know I'm not the only one who once interpreted my mental illness as a personal failing before someone told me otherwise.

You owe it to yourself to seek out other people's stories, statistics, and as much information as you can. The more you know, the more context you can build for whatever it is you're going through and the sooner you can find the proper avenues for help and healing—and feel less alone.

Balance / We all know, logically, that life is about balance, but that

doesn't mean it's easy to put into practice, or that it's always going to
be logistically possible to do so. It's worth aiming for an equal balance
of things that mentally revitalize you and things that tire you out;
otherwise, you'll feel burned out all the time.

If you don't know where to start, make a list of every aspect of your
daily life (such as work, chores, hangouts with friends, sports, sleep,
grocery shopping, etc.) and note whether each activity charges your
~battery~ or leaves you feeling depleted. Be super specific, and be
super honest with yourself! Like, yes, exercise should revitalize you
in theory, but if your current exercise habits are cutting into time with

friends and your sleep schedule, it might actually be depleting you. Once you've got your list, figure out what changes you can make, or what you can add that would help restore some balance to your life. *See also* Prioritize.

Because self-care looks so, so different for everyone, I've asked dozens of people from all walks of life what self-care means to **them**. Their stories are scattered throughout this guide and aren't meant to be prescriptive—they're simply a window into all the intimate ways we take care of ourselves.

Their Care: "I think that women, employees, and parents are all conditioned, to a certain extent, to put ourselves last. I read once that mothers who work are supposed to work as if they don't have children, and parent as if they don't work. That held incredible resonance for me. I lead a department at work, and am expected to do that to a high level while mentoring my staff. At the same time—as if parenting young children wasn't exhausting enough—I have a daughter with special needs, which is really a whole other level. I absolutely put myself and my own needs last much of the time.

"So, to me, self-care is about not putting myself last. It's about being a little selfish and taking time and space for myself, recognizing that doing so will replenish my reserves and keep it together enough to continue facing the day-to-day grind. It's reading a book instead of making lunches, cleaning up the kitchen, or folding the laundry. It's spending time with friends who don't need anything from me but my company. It's creating spaces, however small, where I am not a mother, a wife, a sister, a daughter, a boss, an employee, but just myself."

—**Courtney, 43, Silver Spring, MD**

Bare Minimum /

A lot of the time, self-care is about just finding small ways to feel a little more human. To that end, giving yourself permission to do the bare minimum when you're struggling is a cornerstone of looking after yourself.

Can't get out of bed? Stretch and take a couple of deep breaths. Keep a bottle of water on your nightstand so you can stay hydrated. Having trouble keeping up with hygiene? Next time you feel up for it, stock up on mouthwash, makeup wipes, baby wipes, dry shampoo, and other cleansing items that require less energy than a full shower. Same goes for having granola bars or other ready-to-eat foods on hand for bad days. If you're feeling up for it, try going outside, even if it's just to stand on your front steps and breathe in some fresh air.

Above all, be kind and gentle with yourself.

Their Care: "I'm not recovered from my eating disorder—I don't think I ever will be—but self-care for me is about fighting it every day and learning to live with it. Eating when I don't think I need to. Not walking the long way to work just to burn more calories. Reading if I can concentrate; if not, just watching something that makes me smile inside. Talking to my online friends who 'get it' more than anyone I've met. Spending time with my family. Turning up to work. Getting out of bed when I feel like the world is ending. Remembering to set reminders to brush my teeth and do basic tasks like washing my face."

—Georgie, 18, United Kingdom

Baths / There's no shortage of

ways to turn a bath into a sanctuary,
from bubbles and oils to music
and candles. If you want to elevate
your experience, make a ritual out of
taking relaxing baths with natural sea
salts—the ocean has a long history of being
used for its healing powers. Or you can
just take a long, no-frills soak at the end of
a long day. On top of just being lovely, regular
hot baths have been shown to help lower blood
pressure, ease joint pain, and lower heart rate.

Best-Case Scenarios / When you're stressed or worried

about something, it's easy to picture *all the ways* it can go wrong.
At best, you're kind of a worrywart, and at worst, you're actually
engaging in "catastrophic thinking." It's about as good for your
mental health as it sounds. When you catastrophize (aka ruminate on
worst-case outcomes), you only wind up *more* anxious.

One thing that can help mellow out the impact of all of the worst-
case scenarios that flood your mind is to make yourself picture best-
case outcomes. Say you're freaking out about a presentation you have
to give. Thoughts that you'll fumble over your words or get massive
pit stains will probably come uninvited no matter how hard you try,
but you can balance those images out. What if you wind up knocking
it out of the park, impressing everyone, and looking like a smart,
capable badass?

There's a third option, too: OK-case scenarios. The pessimists or
the realists among us might not be terribly comforted by thinking on

the bright side. Positivity like that doesn't always reach anxious ears. At that point, you can at least walk yourself through some OK-case scenarios. You know, your presentation happens, it's *fine*, a few people don't pay attention and text instead. You make it through. It's not spectacular, but it's not a catastrophe either. *See also* Decatastrophizing.

Body / Our relationships with our bodies can be complicated, to say the least. On the one hand, the ol' meatsack is truly impressive and amazing, but on the other, it can be the site of a lot of pain, trauma, and shame. No matter how you feel about it, though, you're stuck with it for life—so putting effort into treating your body with kindness, respect, and dignity is necessary to cultivate a healthy relationship with it, or at least a peaceful coexistence.

While you can't erase whatever contributes to your contentious relationship with your body—whether it's an illness, past trauma, or overwhelming messages about what your body is supposed to look like or how it's supposed to function—there are little ways you can improve how you relate to your body every day. Some of them will be covered in this book (like loving self-touch or skin care). But short of the physical things you can do, setting some ground rules is an excellent place to start.

Boundaries / You've probably heard about the importance of setting boundaries, but the idea is such a broad and nebulous one that it can be hard to know where to start. We're not talking about building fences to keep out annoying neighbors here. Boundaries are essentially ground rules you put in place—both by communicating them to others and committing to them yourself—to protect your time, values, mood, emotional well-being, comfort, and even safety. They can be big or small, emotional or physical. Without healthy boundaries, it's really difficult to create a safe space for you and your relationships to flourish.

> **Boundaries are essentially ground rules you put in place—both by communicating them to others and committing to them yourself—to protect your time, values, mood, emotional well-being, comfort, and even safety.**

It might be difficult to know off the top of your head what boundaries you need. They're the kind of things you don't recognize until they pop up, you know? But once you start paying attention to the moments you feel uncomfortable, drained, annoyed, backed into a corner, taken advantage of, steamrolled, violated, ignored, or any number of crappy experiences, it'll be hard to *stop* noticing.

Figure out all the ways you're putting others' needs and feelings before your own and how you can start looking out for yourself. Does your friend dump relationship problems on you too much? Set a date for catching up specifically about that stuff, and tell your friend you'd rather not text about it in the meantime. Do you always get stressed out when people borrow your things and don't return them in a timely manner? Stop lending them. Do you find yourself saying yes when you want to say no? Practice saying no without apology or excuse.

Setting boundaries usually involves having a conversation. It can be awkward, but the type of person you *want* in your life will be receptive—so no matter the outcome, it's usually worth it.

THE TEN COMMANDMENTS FOR HAVING A BODY

1

All bodies are good bodies, including yours.

2

You're not required to always like your body,
but you should never punish it.

3

Don't say anything about your body that you
wouldn't say about your best friend's. Don't say
anything bad about bodies, period. (Why do we
talk so much about bodies, anyway?)

4

Take care of your health out of self-respect, not
obligation, and do it in a way you actually enjoy,
not in a way you think you're supposed to.

5

Don't feel pressured to subscribe to any single body
ideology or social "movement." Your relationship with
your body is deeply personal, and movements that are
empowering to some, like body positivity, might be
restrictive and discouraging to you.

6

Tend to aches and pains. Develop an awareness of what muscles you tense and clench. Don't deny yourself relief. Respect your body's limits and don't push them.

7

Do what you need to do to stop body-checking and scrutinizing. You don't have to keep track of numbers.

8

Don't put off life until your body looks a certain way—take that vacation, make that move, buy that outfit.

9

Forgive yourself for the times you're not immune to the pressures society places on your body. Having a good relationship with your body doesn't mean never feeling pressured to make it look a certain way or never being drawn to fads and their promises of transformation; it's about being aware of the world your body exists in and being kind to it.

10

Your body will change, so the respect you cultivate for it can't be conditional. You and your body are in it together for the long haul.

Their Care: "I'm a civil engineer for a local government. I'm very passionate about what I do: saving the environment and serving the public. I loved my job, but found myself regularly working late and on weekends, not taking any time for myself, and taking work success or failure very personally. I completely burned out.

"Self-care for me means settings boundaries and sticking to them. I do not check work email outside of work and only work one weekend per month. I make sure that if I have something planned for an evening (work meeting or hanging out with friends) then the next evening needs to be kept free for me to chill at home. Since setting boundaries, I've found that I can get a lot more done in my leisure time."

—Sara, 33, Washington, DC

Brain Dump / There are two types of people in the world: those who can have a million and one tabs open on their browser and those who can't. I'm the latter. Having too many tabs open—you know, to the point where each individual tab is so tiny that you can't even see its title anymore—makes me feel tense, scattered, and overwhelmed.

Same goes for my brain. Without getting random thoughts out of my head and onto paper—like groceries I need to buy or a TV show I want to recommend to my mom—I feel like I have too many mental tabs open. My solution is to have a brain dump where you can jot down stray thoughts as they occur so that you can revisit them later. If something pops up and I don't have the bandwidth to deal with that thought, into the brain dump it goes. It can be wherever you want—a Google doc, a little notebook, the notes app on your phone. Whatever's most handy.

Brag / Taking pride in yourself and your accomplishments is such a simple way to boost your own serotonin—aka the happy chemical— and yet we don't do it often enough. But there are ways to toot your own horn without being annoying or boastful. If you read the room and know your audience, there's nothing wrong with sharing what you're proud of. Post some fire selfies. #TBT to a project that never got enough recognition. Own your contributions to an important presentation. Dare to say, "Look what I did!"

Breaks / The thing about breaks is that you probably don't need to be convinced that they're good for you. Not only does a lot of evidence point toward breaks being good for productivity, creativity, and general mental well-being, but you can usually just . . . feel it.

But just because, in theory, you know that taking breaks from work throughout the day are acts of good self-care doesn't mean that you have the follow-through to take them on a regular basis. I get it—I know what it's like to have a ton of shit to do, and the thought of taking a break when my to-do list is miles long stresses me out. But honestly, without breaks, you're not going to wind up using your time well anyway, so you may as well let yourself step away for a bit.

The easiest way to *actually do it* is to schedule breaks into your day. Maybe that means putting a midday walk on your calendar or setting an alarm to go off every hour for a five-minute stretch break when you're working on a project. The important thing is to view breaks as more or less unbreakable appointments with yourself that you honor.

Breathe / Controlling your breath through deep breathing is a powerful tool to manage stress and anxiety. There are dozens of guided approaches out there, but you can't go wrong with the classic 4-7-8 exercise: inhale through your nose for four counts, hold for seven counts, exhale through your mouth for eight counts. Repeat until, hopefully, you feel a little better. *See also* Meditation.

Bullet Journaling / A Bullet Journal (aka dot journal) is the perfect lovechild of a planner, diary, and to-do list. How you use one is entirely up to you—the internet is overflowing with how-to guides, Bullet Journal spread ideas, and templates. Bullet Journaling for self-care—having a place to organize and keep track of my life, goals, habits, and feelings—has been invaluable for my mental health.

Dr. Andrea Bonior summed it up best when I talked to her about Bullet Journaling for mental health: "When your life and emotions feel so out of control or chaotic, there is something immensely therapeutic about organizing it into a systematic structure like a Bullet Journal. You lay things out in an aesthetically pleasing way and already it feels more manageable. Like you can really tackle it and make it through. It feels luxurious, too. It's like saying, 'I'm worth it. I'm worth this notebook and the time it takes to turn it into something beautiful.'"

Their Care: "The goal of my habit tracker is to put down things I can do, so I can feel happy seeing the boxes filled in. I have a 'no matter how small' rule for when I'm not doing well. Wrote one sentence? Check on journal. Did half of my yoga routine? Check on exercise. Only meditated for five minutes? Check. And then I can look down, and no matter how awful I feel, at least I got some stuff done and I kept up with my routine.

"This also helps with staying connected to reality and managing my bipolar and dissociative episodes. I tend to disassociate a lot and, as a result, I lose a lot of time and a lot of my memory. I struggle to remember what goes on and that can be really triggering for me. [Habit-tracking] is an easy way for me to look back and figure out what happened by my entries and habits, and it also helps me look out for any warning signs."

—**Olly, 21, Seattle, WA**

Burn Negative Thoughts / Literally. Things people have

said to you that you want to let go, negative self-talk and insecurities, petty and emotional letters you'll never send, thoughts that won't leave you alone . . . write it all down. Then burn it all up. Blow away the ashes and let your problems go with them. That, baby, is called catharsis.

Caffeine / Full disclosure: Like a ton of people, I love to start my morning with a cup of coffee and am known to down cold brew as soon as my midday slump hits. So I'm not going to be the one to tell you to cut caffeine out of your life—but I *will* mention that paying attention to when and how you consume caffeine can be a lifesaver.

For example, if you're anxious—either circumstantially or in general—having caffeine can be like throwing gasoline on a fire. Think about it: caffeine is a stimulant and its effects on your body can be *a lot* like anxiety. You know, racing heartbeat, fidgeting, that kind of thing. Not exactly the sensations that are great to pile on top of preexisting anxiety. So, pay attention and make sure you're not accidentally making yourself feel worse.

If you want your coffee fix without exacerbating anxiety, try cutting your usual cup with decaf. Or go completely decaf—despite popular belief, decaf coffee actually does still have *some* caffeine. Also, there's a whole world of coffee substitutes out there, and tea with only a fraction of the caffeine. Who knows? You might find out that it's the ceremony of drinking coffee that you're attached to, not the actual caffeine or flavor.

Candles / The ritual of burning candles signals to your body that you're chilling out: the snick of the match, the first leap of a flame, the warm halo of light. A candle announces to any room that it's now a *calm zone*. No stressing allowed, only unwinding and enjoying the gentle atmosphere.

The best thing about candles is that if you know where to look—such as discount department store chains—they can be pretty damn affordable. It's an easy go-to gift to give yourself when you need a pick-me-up. Sometimes, you don't even have to *buy* a candle to feel better; taking a break to sniff every candle in Bath & Body Works may be enough to make you feel better.

CBD (Cannabidiol) / CBD has become somewhat of a wellness darling. People claim it will chill you out, relieve your pain, and do, like, a million other things. CBD is one of the many naturally occurring compounds in the hemp plant. THC—the main psychoactive compound found in hemp that most people think of when they think of cannabis—is another one. Unlike medical marijuana products (which are derived from plants with high

concentrations of THC), CBD oil is made from high-CBD, low-THC hemp. Meaning, CBD might provide benefits like relieving your pain or chilling you out—but you don't have to worry about it getting you high.

Research around CBD is still pretty preliminary and more human studies are needed to substantiate the claims of CBD benefits, but anecdotally, plenty of people swear by it, including people who deal with chronic pain, anxiety, movement disorders, and insomnia. It comes in the form of balms, tinctures, vaporizers, capsules, powders, edible gummies and chocolates, and lubes, and will probably be available in a dozen other ways still to come.

Their Care: "I have a subcategory of OCD called body-focused repetitive behavior (BFRB). I have had this disorder since I was eighteen years old. Because of my BFRB, self-care is incredibly important to my overall well-being. I have to be wary of 'down time,' as this is typically when my rituals [take place]. What is perceived in my mind as cathartic (sitting on the couch, watching Netflix, or scrolling through Instagram) can actually lead to my rituals taking over before I realize it. I have a few coping mechanisms in my repertoire that help me to keep my hands and my mind occupied, while still being able to participate in otherwise 'mindless' activities. I've found consuming small doses of CBD has been the most effective."

—Amy, 26, Boston, MA

Celebrate Small Victories / Listen, sometimes doing

your laundry or speaking up for yourself *is* a big deal. Instead of
brushing things off for being small potatoes or beating yourself up for
things you think should be easier, let yourself feel good about the little
ways you show courage and resilience every day. That could mean
patting yourself on the back, treating yourself to a small gift, or even
drawing up a little DIY reward you can tack to your bulletin board.

Change Your Environment / A change in scenery is often

the restart button your brain needs in any number of situations. Maybe
you're angry and irritable, sluggish and foggy, depressed and anxious. Even
if it's as simple as going to a local café to watch Netflix instead of staying
in your musty living room; switch it up to give yourself an opportunity to
move and get out in the world, but without having to *do* anything.

Check-Ins / When was the last time you actually paused to check

in with yourself? I'm not talking about those little moments when you
note that you're thirsty and get a drink, or tired and take a nap—those
are great, but they're not checking in. I'm talking about hosting a one-
on-one with yourself occasionally, maybe once a month or so, to look at
the big-picture stuff. You know, like where you're at in life, how you're
progressing toward goals, and how you're feeling about everything.

This is especially important because we have a tendency to value
instant gratification over long-term pleasure. When we do that and
don't check in with ourselves, it's easy to think things are going well,
while ignoring the important but not always fun things you want
for yourself. So host a little meeting with yourself and ask some
questions: What's been making you happy? What have you been
putting off? Are your goals still things you actually want to achieve?

Clean / A clean space is so calming and affirming, and it's an easy way to show up for yourself—treat yourself like a guest worthy of nice towels and a shining sink. It's also a good form of emergency self-care. If you're pacing around or kind of spiraling and know you should do something but don't know what it should be, try cleaning your bathroom. Don't overthink it; just go. Why? Because it tends to be a relatively short, contained chore—unlike, say, cleaning your closet, which you'll start with good intentions and then lead you to somehow spend seventy-five dollars ordering hangers online before falling asleep on piles of clothes—but it's just long enough to help you gain clarity on what to do next, leave you feeling accomplished, and basically press the reset button when you can't concentrate on anything else.

Cloud Watching / So many outdoor activities require movement: hiking, swimming, even just taking a walk around the block. And while movement is good, do you know what else is good sometimes? *Not moving.* Especially when you're depressed. Enter cloud watching, the underrated activity from our childhoods that requires nothing but lying in the grass and watching the sky and breathing fresh air.

Cognitive Distortions / Our brains are wired to make sense of things, drawing connections between thoughts, ideas, actions, and consequences. But sometimes in an effort to do that, our brains are straight-up wrong, negative, or misleading in ways that impact our mental health. Cognitive behavioral therapists call these instances "cognitive distortions" and teach us to battle them with CBT techniques. In order to utilize exercises and techniques in this book, you have to start with understanding what you're up against, and how our thoughts can work for *or* against us.

Cognitive distortions are the main target of cognitive behavioral therapy (CBT), an action-oriented type of talk therapy meant to teach you how to recognize and correct unhealthy thinking patterns that have a negative impact on your mental health. Tips throughout this book will help you learn to address these unhealthy thinking patterns, but first you have to learn how to identify them!

Here is a quick crash course on a few of the mental traps we can all fall into:

- **FILTERING:** viewing the world with blue-tinted glasses. When you filter, you only focus on the negative—and that can distort your perception of reality.

- **POLARIZED THINKING:** thinking in black and white. With this distortion, you view things in extremes, leaving no room for shades of gray. Something is either good or evil, perfect or a failure, amazing or horrible.

- **OVERGENERALIZATION:** drawing a conclusion from a limited number of experiences. For example, you get a bad grade on a difficult math test and decide that you must be bad at all math.

- **JUMPING TO CONCLUSIONS:** thinking you have the ability to read minds and tell the future. It's *wild* how often we think we know what someone is thinking, what they're going to do, or how things will turn out based on . . . well, usually nothing.

- **CATASTROPHIZATION:** always anticipating the worst possible outcome. *See also* Best-Case Scenarios.

- **PERSONALIZATION:** taking everything as a reflection of or response to you. Everyone in the world is the center of their own universe and has their own motivation and inner world. But when you personalize something, you take it to heart and assume that it is all about you.

- **FALLACY OF CONTROL:** either believing that nothing is in your control or that *everything* is. Rather than viewing the world as a complex place where you're subject to both choice and happenstance, you find yourself believing that you're either a victim of fate and circumstance or entirely responsible for everything, such as your own happiness and the happiness of others.

- **FALLACY OF FAIRNESS:** mistakenly believing that every situation should be determined by what is fair. Life isn't fair (who else heard that a million times as a child?) and when you expect it to be, you wind up feeling angry, resentful, or even hopeless.

- **BLAMING:** holding other people responsible for your feelings and not taking accountability for your own emotions and reactions. When someone's actions make you feel a certain way, it doesn't always mean they did something *wrong*—it may just mean they triggered a vulnerability of yours that has nothing to do with them. And that's something to hold yourself accountable for, not them.

- **EMOTIONAL REASONING:** mistaking your feelings for fact. When you engage in emotional reasoning, you think, *I feel this way, so it must be true.*

- **FALLACY OF CHANGE:** pinning happiness on the expectation that someone else can or will change if you're patient enough. Or, you know, if you bug them enough.

And these are only some of the most common mental traps. Learning to recognize what's going on when you're struggling with a negative or harmful thought is the first step to addressing it, so be on the alert for these thinking patterns.

Coloring Books / You're never too old for the relaxing
satisfaction of taking colored pencil to paper and making something
beautiful. Or, you know, something really ugly. You don't have to be a
talented artist to color. You don't even have to stay inside the lines.

Color Therapy / If you've ever had a power outfit you wear
when you need confidence or found yourself overwhelmed by a
beautiful painting, chances are you know that colors can evoke
feelings and energy. One of the easiest ways to take advantage of that
is to work certain colors into your life, whether in your space or your
wardrobe. Wear red to stay grounded, orange to stimulate creativity,
yellow and gold for strength and joy, green for growth, blue for
increased communication and logic, and purple for mysticism—or
whatever personal associations you have with each color. It's not an
exact science. Who knows if it'll really work, but even if it just sets up
a self-fulfilling prophecy, you're still reaping the benefits.

Communicate / Even though self-care isn't inherently selfish, it
can help a lot to communicate to your loved ones what your self-care
looks like so they're in the loop. Without the proper context, people
might misinterpret your self-care as disrespectful or as a cry for help,
or find it just plain weird. For example, if a big part of your self-care
involves getting to bed at a certain time, it doesn't hurt to tell your
friends that *that* is the reason you're never down for late-night plans,
not because you don't want to spend time with them.

Complain Less / Complaining is essentially the noisy cousin

of rumination, aka thinking about something in endless circles. And ruminating on negative thoughts takes a big toll on your mental health in the long run, making you more susceptible to depression and anxiety. Don't hold stuff in, by any means, but make an effort to express those negative thoughts once and move on—or at least keep an eye on when revisiting an issue again becomes unproductive.

Watch out for actual complaining disguised as something else— venting with friends over brunch, nitpicking to be "helpful," anything that starts with "I just think it's funny how . . ." Need help getting started? Turn to your conversations with friends, phone calls with your parents, or journal entries from the past few weeks. What subjects keep crawling their way up your throat or out of your pen? It can feel good to rant in the moment—and it *can* be good for you, in moderation—but if there's something you can't stop rehashing, it might be time to loosen your grip. *See also* Rumination.

Compliment / Compliment yourself and other people. A few

genuine, kind words go a long way and there's a specific kind of joy attached to watching someone's face light up (or hey, turn bright red) at a compliment.

HOW TO GIVE A
GOOD COMPLIMENT:

❊ Be specific. Generic compliments that anyone could receive sound half-assed at best and seem like lip service at worst.

❊ Offer compliments freely and without expectation of anything in return.

❊ Don't say anything you don't actually mean—fake compliments are worse than no compliments at all.

❊ Bury a compliment in a conversation to make it easier to receive. Accepting compliments is hard for a lot of people, so, depending on whom you're talking to, something like, "That presentation was incredible—is public speaking a hobby of yours?" might be better than just "That presentation was soooo good."

❊ Skip compliments related to someone's looks and body unless you have a close enough relationship to know what is and isn't appropriate. And maybe not even then, because you never *really* know.

❊ Don't focus on compliments that are about how a person is useful to you. Comments like "You're a great listener, you're so generous, you're always there when I need you" are all lovely things to say, but they emphasize what a person can give you. Focus instead on qualities that just make you grateful to exist in the same timeline as this person—their humor, their passion, their creativity, their optimism, or their kindness.

Cook / Being in the kitchen engages all of your senses. And there's something incredibly soothing and rewarding about watching a bunch of ingredients become something delicious that nourishes you. When you start with the barest of ingredients, cooking feels like creating something out of nothing.

Their Care: "My dad passed away when I was eighteen and my mental health really plummeted. I started hallucinating. I couldn't tell if I was awake or asleep. I had to count my fingers to tell if I was dreaming or not, and I'd do it ten to twenty times a day. I more or less just became a black hole of a person. I was only officially diagnosed with PTSD in 2018, but I've known that's what it was since I was nineteen or twenty.

"Because my trauma stalled me at eighteen, self-care means learning how to be a grown-up in the way that I was supposed to while I was imploding. For me, that's things like learning how to cook for myself, learning to bake for enjoyment (I'm good at it!! Who knew???), learning how to determine who is a friend and who isn't, and just generally relearning how to be a person. I lost some really crucial years (made more complicated as a queer woman, since you also lose crucial childhood and teen years) so self-care for me involves building a life."

—Maggie, 23, Toronto, Canada

Coping Mechanisms / The worst thing about the best

coping mechanisms—and by best, I mean the most distracting, most satisfying, quickest, or easiest—is that some of them aren't very good for you in excess. Unless you're a supremely well-adjusted person, these might mean drinking, shopping, binge-watching, or eating comfort foods.

While most coping mechanisms are fine in moderation, it's important to keep an eye on whether you rely on the arguably detrimental ones. Even if you don't think you have a "problem," it's never a bad idea to check in with yourself to see if, first and foremost, a behavior *actually* makes you feel better.

For example, as a generally anxious person, I find that alcohol can be a seemingly great social lubricant. There was a time when getting drunk got me through parties, made me feel more charming, and empowered me to talk to more people. But once I got real with myself, I had to acknowledge that I experienced *more* anxiety as a result of drinking. After a night of drinking, an anxiety spiral would hit. *Was I annoying? Did I say anything weird? Was I misreading signs from that girl I was flirting with and making a total fool of myself?*

The moral of the story is that a lot of coping mechanisms exacerbate the very issues we're trying to treat, but making that call requires honest reflection.

If you or someone you love is struggling with an addiction, check out the resources available on the Substance Abuse and Mental Health Services Administration (SAMHSA) website or talk to a representative on their free, confidential, 24-7 national helpline by calling 1-800-662-HELP. (And if you're not in the US, your national mental health services will likely point you in the direction of a similar resource.)

Their Care: "A lot of what is stereotypically and capitalistically deemed self-care can actually be quite destructive for me. Let's just say that during my more challenging depressive episodes, I tend to *really* overspend on toiletries and chocolate to pamper myself, and then I am ultimately just more depressed, but this time with a face mask."

—Merritt, 24, Salt Lake City, UT

Creativity / If you're a creative person—whatever that means to you—nourishing that creative energy is a huge part of taking care of your spirit. Otherwise, I don't think it's an exaggeration to say that you're neglecting an important part of you, and that neglect could have a profound effect on your well-being. Poet Mary Oliver once wrote in *Blue Pastures*, a collection of prose pieces, "The most regretful people on earth are those who felt the call to creative work, who felt their own creative power restive and uprising, and gave to it neither power nor time." If these words speak to you, don't forget them.

Cry / If you've ever wondered why crying can feel so cathartic, a reasonable scientific explanation is that it actually releases endorphins, the little feel-good hormones that you also get from exercise and sex. Which, cool.

Anyone who's ever gone a while without crying and then finally *let it out* knows the sweet, sweet feeling of release. It's like you get plugged up when you don't clean out the tear ducts occasionally. (My favorite way to cry is in public on the subway while listening to dramatic music. This is a strong choice for me because (1) I live in New York City, where it's pretty commonplace and no one will look twice at the crying girl, and (2) it makes me feel like a tragic heroine in an indie movie when really I'm just crying because I can't stop overthinking something my boss said and I need a nap. But follow your heart.)

If you've ever wondered why crying can feel so cathartic, a reasonable scientific explanation is that it actually releases endorphins, the little feel-good hormones that you also get from exercise and sex.

Crystals / Crystals are hardly new—in fact, some are downright

ancient—but they've exploded into the mainstream in a blast of light, color, and good vibes. No longer confined to specialty new age shops, crystals are finding their way into the hands, pockets, and altars of a new generation.

For the uninitiated, the idea behind crystals is that, as old remnants of the earth, they have absorbed energy, wisdom, and healing properties through the years, and that by interacting with them, we can benefit from that energy.

Crystals don't have to be that deep, though. They have a straight-up aesthetic appeal and you can just enjoy them for what they are: enchanting stones and gems that come in endless alluring shapes

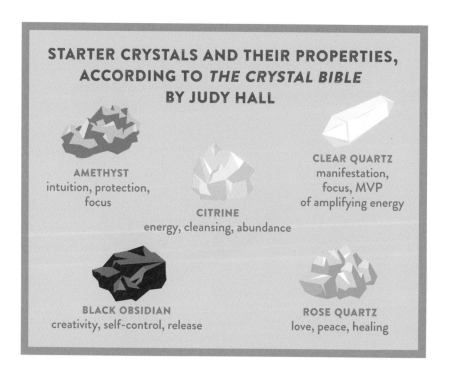

STARTER CRYSTALS AND THEIR PROPERTIES, ACCORDING TO *THE CRYSTAL BIBLE* BY JUDY HALL

AMETHYST
intuition, protection, focus

CITRINE
energy, cleansing, abundance

CLEAR QUARTZ
manifestation, focus, MVP of amplifying energy

BLACK OBSIDIAN
creativity, self-control, release

ROSE QUARTZ
love, peace, healing

and colors. Even disregarding their properties, there's no denying that there is something magical about them.

A good middle ground is using crystals as lovely reminders for intentions. You don't have to believe that carrying around a hunk of rose quartz will magically attract love to you, but you *can* utilize it as a physical reminder to be positive and compassionate.

Curiosity / Curiosity can get you so many places. It can direct you toward new and exciting things, smooth over awkward conversations by giving you questions to ask, add a little childlike wonder to your life, and even boost happiness.

But most importantly, in terms of self-care, cultivating a little curiosity—about the world, about the future—can be a lifeline. A therapist once told me, as we were talking about the rising of hopelessness that finds its way under my skin sometimes, "You don't have to be hopeful about what's to come, you just have to be curious."

> **Cultivating a little curiosity— about the world, about the future— can be a lifeline.**

Dance / If you think the advice to dance like no one is watching is cheesy and overplayed, it's probably because you have never before danced like no one is watching. Dancing is a singular, liberating way of saying *fuck it* to basic socially acceptable behavior: moving only when you're supposed to move, not drawing attention to yourself, not looking stupid. Dancing, on the other hand, is flailing your body around with abandon to a song that has needled into your brain and sent shocks out to every nerve. In public or in private, dancing is a satisfying, freeing, wonderful, silly antidote for low spirits.

D

Daydream / It's important to have a space of your own, but the reality is, not everyone has the privilege of that being a physical space. Maybe you have a roommate, maybe your whole house is toxic or even dangerous, or maybe you just need to escape. Dipping into a fantasyland, or daydreaming, is a treat that offers respite and comfort of the self-soothing variety, an indulgent dessert of self-care.

Decatastrophizing / Sometimes, a worst-case scenario pops into your brain and sinks its claws in, and no amount of counteracting with positive or mediocre outcomes will loosen its grip. Well, there's a CBT tool for dealing with catastrophizing, too. (Isn't CBT great? It's like the Swiss Army knife of mental wellness.) Decatastrophizing, also known as the "what if" technique, is the act of playing out the scenario you fear.

What does that look like? Here's a conversation I had with myself recently when rumors of upcoming company-wide layoffs were swirling at my work:

> *What if I lose my job in the layoffs?*
> *Well, I would be really hurt and upset.*
> *OK, and then what?*
> *I'd lose my health insurance and wouldn't be able to afford my antidepressants.*
> *OK, and then what?*
> *Then I'd be too depressed to look for another job and, eventually, my savings would run out and I would go broke.*
> *OK, then what?*

I'd probably have to move back home to my parents' house.
OK, then what?
I'd mope around and binge-watch Netflix.
OK, then what?
I guess I would probably get bored and maybe try to do some
*   freelance work.*

And on and on.

When you employ decatastrophization, you're basically walking yourself gently to the realization that, no matter what your gremlin brain is telling you, things will be OK. Obviously, this doesn't work if you're catastrophizing about, say, dying in a plane crash (although, I guess you could still play *And then what? And then I'd become a ghost and get to haunt all my enemies*), but many of our fears, even the big ones, can be de-escalated to the point of survival and rehabilitation.

Oh, and spoiler alert: I did lose that job. And things turned out OK.

D

Declutter / Ditch things that aren't serving you anymore. If you have things in your closet or in your home that make you feel worse when you see them—such as clothes that you plan on fitting into again "one day," or mementos of an old relationship—toss them. Of course, it's worth acknowledging that decluttering doesn't come easy to everyone. It sure doesn't come easy to me—I hoard meaningless and useless things the way a dragon guards gold, and I need help when it comes to cleaning out my life.

An excellent guide? Marie Kondo's *The Life-Changing Magic of Tidying Up*, her book outlining her beloved organizing method, which boils down to getting rid of anything that doesn't "spark joy." Beyond this philosophy, the book is also filled with little tips, such as picking storage containers you'll actually utilize and decanting household products to reduce the "noise" that branded products add to our spaces.

Deepen Relationships / Good friendships are comfortable and reliable—you can sit in them like cozy sweaters, enjoy your traditions and routines, and feel safe and secure in your closeness. But with that familiarity might come stagnation, and you might forget the joy of new discoveries and understandings of the people you love.

Ask questions. Explore new experiences and situations together. Meet the people who are important to them. Put your relationships to the test with the understanding that a full, long-lasting relationship means knowing the ugly bits as well.

And don't forget to share about yourself, too: insecurities and dreams and fears and dark corners of yourself that don't regularly get to see the light of day. There's a thrill to letting yourself know and be known.

GOOD FRIENDSHIPS
ARE COMFORTABLE
AND RELIABLE—YOU
CAN SIT IN THEM LIKE
COZY SWEATERS, ENJOY
YOUR TRADITIONS AND
ROUTINES, AND FEEL SAFE
AND SECURE IN YOUR
CLOSENESS.

Ditch the Brave Face / Do you know how exhausting it is
to pretend to be OK? When we're in pain, emotional or physical, it's
wild how much energy we put into making our experiences palatable
and easier to digest for others. For example, we push through pain
to avoid canceling plans, we smile and say we're doing well when
people ask, we sanitize our crises and episodes so they don't sound
like a big deal. We've been taught that it's admirable and noble to
be unwavering and strong in the face of adversity, but whom does
that help? Not us. In fact, it might hurt us. We don't have to expend
energy on making other people comfortable with our pain. The
people who are worth our time will be supportive if we occasionally
need to let it out.

Their Care: "I'm a Black, queer, gender-fluid person who is
constantly read as female and I live in a city where it feels like near-
constant erosion just to survive. 'Self-care' as a term kind of stresses me
out at this point, because I think of travel and spa treatments and other
expensive experiences that I just can't afford.

"What resonates more with me is just giving myself a fucking break
sometimes, or allowing myself to enjoy and indulge in the things my spirit
keeps returning to. I've gotten less patient with institutional bullshit to
protect myself. Self-care for me recently has looked like dropping classes
when I am the only person of color and when the vibe feels off. It has
looked like walking out of work meetings when people are being offensive.
It has looked like being honest with my boss about the abysmal treatment
I experience from cisgender, white coworkers. It looks like changing my
hair and playing with my gender presentation."

—**Ash, 29, Brooklyn, NY**

Doctor / Find one!

Doctor / Find one! Having a doctor you love comes in handy in so many ways—including when you need a referral to help treat depression, anxiety, stress, or any host of mental health–adjacent issues. If you don't have a general doctor, make a point of getting one. One thing I've learned about scheduling my doctor's appointments—which I hate doing—is that you just have to rip the Band-Aid off.

It's so easy to put off going to the doctor for routine checkups when you're in fine health. No one is holding you accountable or reminding you that it's been a *liiittle* too long since your last physical, dental, or eye exam. And life is busy!

But honestly, putting off making those appointments can spiral pretty easily. As silly as it sounds, if it's been a while since you've been to a doctor, it can be hard to get back in the saddle. I don't know about you, but I definitely feel a bit nervous and embarrassed crawling back after a long absence. Like, "Oh heeeey, yeah, it *has* been forever since my last dental cleaning, and no, I'm still not flossing."

On the subject of doctors, though, I don't want to pretend like finding a doctor you love is easy. Testing out different providers until you find one you click with isn't a luxury that everyone has. Even more difficult is finding a doctor who respects and understands your needs—for example, if you need a doctor who is queer- and trans-friendly, fat-positive, or who actually has experience treating patients of color.

There are resources (such as the Gay and Lesbian Medical Association provider directory) that can point you in the right direction, but if you're limited by insurance coverage, you might have to spend some time brushing up on your patient advocacy skills. It's not ideal, but if you're stuck with a subpar doc, learning how to stand up for yourself and get what you need out of the medical system can be necessary. Luckily, the internet is full of guides to advocating for yourself at the doctor, written by people who have been there and by doctors alike.

A few doctors to think about scheduling appointments with:

✔ **YOUR GENERAL PRACTITIONER** for your annual physical.

✔ **YOUR DENTIST.** I hate to be the bearer of bad news, but according to the American Dental Association, you should probably get cleanings every six months.

✔ **YOUR OPTOMETRIST.** The American Optometric Association recommends a visit to the eye doctor every two years for general eye health, but depending on your history or if you notice a change in your vision, once a year might be more fitting.

✔ **YOUR GYNECOLOGIST** (if you have a vagina). You've probably heard that you should get a Pap test yearly, but good news: the average suggestion is once every three years now, according to the American College of Obstetricians and Gynecologists. Even if you're not due for a Pap smear, though, there could be other reasons to hit up a gynecologist. Are you due for an STD/STI test or a check-in about birth control, maybe?

✔ **YOUR DERMATOLOGIST.** Maybe you have a goal of taking better care of your skin or are due for a skin exam (mole check, people!)—either way, put it on the cal.

You might also want to schedule non-yearly appointments you've been meaning to get around to, like with a therapist or another specialist about a problem that's been bugging you forever. While you're on a roll, you might as well.

D

Done List / Sometimes energy is low and the number of things you need to do is high, and that can be an especially demoralizing combination. To take the pressure off, a done list is a handy hack. Instead of creating a gigantic to-do list you have to tackle, add things to a done list as you accomplish them. Whereas slowly chipping away at a long to-do list can be discouraging and overwhelming, watching your done list grow gratifies you.

You should include everything on your done list. On bad days, my done list might look something like this:

1. Made bed

2. Took meds

3. Brushed teeth

4. Took shower and put on fresh clothes

5. Caught up on texts I owed people

6. Ate three solid meals

If you don't deal with depression or something adjacent, this might look really silly to you. But if you do, you know that on some days, these are all Herculean tasks. Enumerating them in a list, no matter how small or seemingly insignificant, is a good way to assert, *I took care of myself the best I could today. I'm doing the best I can.*

Do Not Disturb / Sometimes you need to put safety guards and rules in place to keep your habits at bay or to protect your self-care time. The do not disturb feature on your phone is an underrated tool for this. Turn it on before bed so the group chat blowing up doesn't disturb your sleep, or if you know notifications are likely to distract you from reading (or whatever). If you want to commit to taking care of yourself, you have to take a preemptive strike against things you know will get in the way.

Doodle / Carry around a sketchbook or notebook with you that you can whip out when you need a distraction or something to do with your hands. You can also commit to doing a doodle a day. Whether you're an artist or not, carving out a bit of time to scribble anything— hell, even a boxy house with the sun peeking out of the corner of your paper like we all used to do—is a guaranteed moment to yourself, every day.

Speaking of distractions . . .
Distracting yourself from your problems and emotions gets kind of a bad rep, but sometimes it is *so needed*. There are always going to be times when an emotion is too much to sit with, when there isn't any immediate action you can take, or when you just need to do whatever you can to *feel better*. That's when it's time to go to the movies, watch a feel-good show, immerse yourself in a video game, go out dancing, *whatever*. These are just suggestions—it's up to you to decide what you really need.

Dream Journal / Tuning in to your dreams is an easy way to tap into your ~unconscious mind~ and get in touch with what's going on with you emotionally. You don't have to run out and buy a dream dictionary or anything—if you have a gut feeling that a dream is

trying to tell you something, you're probably right. At the very least, *how* you interpret your dreams is your translation of your intuitions. Try keeping a dream journal if that'll help you dive in. Even if you're not suddenly overcome with discoveries of your unconscious mind, carving out time in the morning to write is a mindful and relaxing way to start your day.

Drive / There are few spaces that provide the same magic you can find inside a car. It's private without being isolated. It offers both shelter and freedom. It is your traveling scream room, your portable cry box, your own personal concert venue. With all that at your disposal, sometimes you just need to get on the road and drive.

Drop the Plot / Just like with cognitive distortions, our brains are hardwired to create meaning, but a lot of the time, that's not very good for us. When things happen, you might find yourself weaving stories—about what someone was thinking when they hurt you, about patterns in the things that have gone wrong, about what you think should and shouldn't happen, about what you do and don't deserve. You can get carried away analyzing life events like plot lines in a movie—but our lives aren't movies! They're way too messy and unpredictable for that.

Trying to make narrative sense out of your life will only cause frustration and rumination. If you catch yourself trying to guess what other people are thinking or why something happened, bring the focus back to you and ask yourself what triggered the feeling (of insecurity, of anger, of whatever) in the first place.

Eat / When life gets hard, our relationship with food can be a complicated one. Maybe you lose your appetite completely or maybe you're more voracious than ever. Or perhaps without the energy to cook, you end up prioritizing convenience over nutrition. Whatever it is, eating well when you're depressed is no simple task.

But not eating (or eating foods that make you feel physically worse) is going to leave you feeling depleted and make it that much harder to do all the other forms of self-care.

WAYS TO NOURISH YOUR BODY EVEN WHEN IT'S DIFFICULT:

❋ Utilize good days to prep some emergency frozen meals for your extra-bad days.

❋ Minimize the number of dishes you'll have to wash to make mealtime a little easier. The internet is full of one-pot and one pan dump meals.

❋ Remember that not everything you eat has to look like a socially acceptable meal. If the thought of even making a sandwich is too much, no one's going to come banging on your door to scold you if you decide to eat a few slices of turkey, some cheese, and some lettuce without actually assembling it into a sandwich.

❋ Get grocery delivery or a meal kit service. There was a time when I was living off nothing but FreshDirect salads. Would it have been cheaper to assemble my own damn salads? Sure. But I didn't have the bandwidth to do that, and the other choice was ordering food on Seamless, which was even more expensive.

❋ Ask for help. Ask a loved one to pick you up some food, or to help you cook, or to help you feel better in other ways so you can go back to doing it yourself. Never be afraid to ask.

Their Care: "I am a US Army veteran and I was diagnosed with binge-eating disorder and depression while I was in the service. Together they sometimes really get you stuck in a vicious cycle. You have days where you just don't want to do anything. You don't want to get out of bed. Or you can't stop eating. And you frustrate yourself so much thinking about how 'bad' of a person you are for thinking this way or not getting out of bed that it just makes everything worse.

So my version of self-care is allowing myself to have these days. To pull out the Netflix and warm heated blankets. For my eating disorder, I allow myself to eat what food I am craving and try to be satisfied with it. I allow myself to have weakness and work through it."

—Amanda, 25, Virginia

Educate / ~Self-help books~ get kind of a bad rep—a lot of them are too sparkly and cheesy or based on pseudoscience, or make life-changing promises that are impossible to keep. But a lot of them are genuinely helpful and educational. You probably don't think of your mental health as something you can continuously learn more about—at least not in the same way you learn in school or develop new skills through a career—but . . . why not?

If you need a place to start, Dr. Guy Winch's *Emotional First Aid* is one of my go-to recommendations. It employs one of my favorite philosophies, which is that mental health should be looked after with the same care and urgency as physical health. Dr. Winch outlines various "emotional wounds" we all sustain day to day, goes over long-term consequences of each, and provides "treatments."

Many of the treatments involve making lists (such as journaling about your self-defeating behaviors that might be sabotaging your life, or listing people you'd like to get to know better to identify potential opportunities for social connectedness when you're lonely) or participating in exercises (such as one to help you increase your tolerance of compliments when you have low self-esteem or one that trains you to change your perspective when you can't stop overthinking something). He provides clear and detailed guided instructions; even the skeptic in me couldn't deny that following them made me feel a little stronger and a little more resilient every time I put in the effort. *See also* Further Reading (page 227).

Their Care: "I work in neuroscience, and have been working on projects surrounding neurotransmitters as an act of self-interest mainly—I don't really *like* neuro, but I have PTSD as a result of sexual assault, which developed further into clinical depression accompanied by general anxiety disorder, and it helps to educate myself about why my brain acts the way it does."

—Sage, 24, Philadelphia, PA

Emergency Self-Care Kit /

As much as I like to think this book is a self-care kit in and of itself, sometimes we need a tangible "break in case of emergency" box filled with a bunch of feel-good solutions. You can call it whatever you want: your happy box, your chill-out box, your self-care package, or your coping toolkit. Take the time to craft it lovingly so you have positive associations with it and keep it somewhere easy to access. For extra credit, you can even make a mini traveling one to keep in your bag.

SOME THINGS YOU MIGHT WANT TO PUT IN YOUR EMERGENCY SELF-CARE KIT:

- **REMINDERS OF YOUR SUPPORT SYSTEM:** letters from loved ones, pictures, transcripts of compliments or nice texts you've received

- **COPING TOOLS AND THERAPY MATERIALS:** worksheets, reminders of CBT or DBT tools and exercises, sensory items

- **MEANS OF SELF-EXPRESSION:** journals, sketchbooks, coloring books, art supplies

- **CALMING AND DISTRACTING ITEMS:** candles, lotions, essential oils, favorite books

- **ENCOURAGING QUOTES AND MANTRAS**

- **RESOURCES:** the names and numbers of local resources and support lines in your community

- **BASICALLY, WHATEVER YOU WANT!**

Expecto Patronum / If you're a fan of the classic children's series Harry Potter, you can skip this next little primer. But if you opted out or just need a little refresher, I got you. In Harry Potter, there are creatures called Dementors—grotesque, skeletal, hooded beings—who can sense and feed on positive feelings, draining their victims of all happiness. On top of being terrifying magical specters, they were also stand-ins for author J. K. Rowling's struggle with depression. They suck the joy out of every room they enter, drowning all in their vicinity in hopelessness and despair.

The spell that drives Dementors away is *expecto patronum*, cast by conjuring up a supremely happy memory. Powered by that joyous image, the witches and wizards of the world could banish Dementors.

Depression, sadly, does not work like that. If witches and wizards have trouble coming up with a happy memory with Dementors staring them down, it's doubly hard to scrape one up when you're drowning in depression. But there's something to be said for reminding yourself—when you're at your worst and happiness seems far, far out of reach—that you're capable of it. That you've felt it before. Sitting with memories can help with that.

Close your eyes and reach back to a moment you felt loved, cared for, powerful, happy, or calm. What did it feel like, what did it look like? If you have a hard time getting there, it's OK. Just like when casting *expecto patronum*, sometimes you have to try again with another memory.

CLOSE YOUR EYES
AND REACH BACK TO
A MOMENT YOU FELT
LOVED, CARED FOR,
POWERFUL, HAPPY,
OR CALM.

Fandom / Fandom—a community of those devoted to something
like a show, movie, book, band, or celebrity—is now part of the
mainstream lexicon, not the whispered subculture it once was. Yet,
despite its recognition, people who don't participate are quick to
have opinions on fandom anyway: that it's a waste of time, that it's
unhealthy escapism. But anyone who loves something enough to
consider themselves part of its fandom knows that it's far from that.

The best thing about fandom is that it provides an opportunity to
have feelings about something other than your own life. It's a bubble
of fictional people, relationships, events, and problems that you get
to delight in. Your life is going to shit? Well, that's no fun. Your

favorite character's life is going to shit? OK, also bad, but also weirdly entertaining and enthralling, and you're allowed to scream about it as dramatically as you want!

Participating in a fandom also wraps up many self-care habits in a compelling package. It's inherently social—you need people to share the experience with, even if it's only in comments on their fan fiction or in mentions on Twitter. It also encourages creativity. Hello, fan fiction, fan art, and cosplaying.

I am a firm believer that the passion of fans can be healing AF. Loving something so much that you want to yell about it with other people, create theories about it, ship it, create fan-works—well, that's the type of stuff that will clear your skin and add years onto your life. *See also* Internet Friends.

Feel Your Feelings / It can be tempting to think of self-care as something that should make you feel better. And it's not *not* that. But sometimes shitty feelings aren't really problems that can be solved, and it's good to be aware of how coping mechanisms—even seemingly healthy ones—can keep us from doing the hard work of sitting with our grief, anger, guilt, or shame. These feelings need to be felt and not rushed through or ignored.

Their Care: "In the past year I endured a breakup of a long-term relationship, another breakup of a relationship I thought was going somewhere, the loss of my grandma, the loss of the dog I raised from puppyhood, and countless rejections from job applications and interviews. At times, self-care is being alone and letting myself feel all of the things

I've endured over the past year. I've dealt with so much pain and rejection, and sometimes I just need to feel bad for myself.

"I was rejected from my dream job about two weeks after I ended a long-term relationship. I cried for hours, and then watched the series finale of *Lost* to induce more crying because I needed to feel terrible for a while. Then, when I was done crying, I bought a bomb-ass romper, went to a brewery with my friend, and played yard games to build up my confidence. But I couldn't do that without first feeling all of the pain and anxiety."

—**Allison, 24, Kansas City, MO**

Fidget Toys / So many people swear by fidget and sensory items, which—depending on who is utilizing them—can provide distraction or focus or both. You might know them as toys like fidget spinners and thinking putty, but the concept of sensory items is hardly new. For example, Baoding balls—also known as Chinese meditation balls—have long been used in a similar way as Western stress balls. You'd probably recognize Baoding balls if you saw them—they're metal balls small enough to hold in one hand that chime with movement. Rotating them in your palm might improve finger dexterity, relax the hand, or help muscle strength and mobility.

Like Baoding balls, modern sensory toys aren't useful for just one thing. Those with ADHD might find them helpful in focusing their attention; people with body-focused repetitive behaviors might use them to busy their hands so they can't pick or scratch their skin; anyone can add them to their meditation practice, especially if they have a hard time doing nothing.

Fika / In Sweden, the twice-daily coffee break known as *fika* is a cherished tradition. If you're a coffee drinker, you might think you do the same, but fika is more than simply grabbing coffee. It's about taking time during the day to slow down, take a step away from life's chaos, and enjoy simple pleasures. I don't know about you, but this does not sound like how I usually grab my coffee—in a rush, to go, in between meetings, or at my desk going over emails. Obviously, for Swedes, fika is just a regular part of everyday life—but for the rest of us, fika is a custom worth stealing.

As Anna Brones and Johanna Kindvall write in their book *Fika: The Art of the Swedish Coffee Break*, "Functioning as both a verb and a noun, the concept of fika is simple. It is the moment that you take a break, often with a cup of coffee, but alternatively with tea, and find a baked good to pair with it. You can do it alone, you can do it with friends. You can do it at home, in a park, or at work. But the essential thing is that you do it, that you make time to take a break: that's what fika is all about."

Finish Something Small / Do a chore, answer an email,

find a stamp and actually mail the bill. Choose one thing on your to-do list that you know you can actually finish, and then do that thing. Bonus points if it's something that's been haunting your to-do list for weeks.

Five Senses Exercise / When you need to practice a bit

of mindfulness quickly and ground yourself—whether from anxiety, stress, or another emotion—try the five senses exercise, which can be done pretty much anywhere. Like it sounds, it is bringing attention to the senses you're experiencing, one by one, in the moment.

5 First, notice five things you can see around you, especially things you wouldn't normally take the time to notice.

4 Then, four things you can feel, such as the breeze from an open window, your cat snoozing at your side, and the softness of your shirt fabric.

3 Then, bring your awareness to three things you can hear that might otherwise blend into the background.

2 Then, two things you can smell, pleasant or unpleasant.

1 And last, one thing you can taste, even if it's as simple as zoning in on how you might describe the taste of the inside of your mouth.

Fix Something Small and Irritating / The drawer

that always gets jammed or the fitted sheet that won't stay on your damn mattress might not seem like big deals—they're, in fact, very small deals. But if you have to force that drawer open or adjust your sheets on a daily basis, that is puncturing your life with small irritations until you're carrying around a broiling undercurrent of annoyance.

When you run into problems that need fixing, even if you don't have time in the moment to do so, write it down. Keep a list. Next time you have a free moment, or need to accomplish something small, you'll know where to start.

Flowers / I'm going to let you in on a secret: *You can buy flowers for yourself.* You don't have to wait for someone to give them to you!! That might seem obvious to you, but it did *not* to me, and it's life-changing. Fresh flowers in your space brings automatic color and aroma—and OK, a little whimsy and romance, too.

Alternatively, if you think sending yourself flowers is a little too extra (it's not), you can recruit a friend to do a swap where you both send *each other* flowers instead and everyone wins.

Forgive Others / Forgiveness is tricky. We know *in theory* that
holding grudges and dwelling on pain and wrongdoing isn't exactly
great for us. But this logical attitude can be hard to tap into when
we've been hurt. Nothing will invalidate our feelings faster than
someone telling us to ~just forgive~ someone and move on.

But forgiveness can be a gift of self-compassion to yourself without
even taking into consideration the other person. Letting go of anger,
betrayal, and hurt doesn't have to mean accepting what someone did
to you or saying that they were right—it's just about exorcising those
negative feelings from your body so they don't weigh so heavily on *you*.
If that sounds easier said than done, you're not the only one who feels
this way: Forgiveness is a skill that often takes time and effort, and
many people benefit from achieving it with the help of a professional.
Consider seeking the help of a therapist or counselor if you find
yourself unable to let something go on your own. *See also* Therapy.

Forgive Yourself for Your Mistakes / You're human
and you're bound to mess up. Don't beat yourself up for a decision
that turned out to be the wrong one. Your decision probably made the
most sense with the data available to you at the time. And as therapist
Dr. Ryan Howes once told me, "When you forgive yourself for your
past decisions, you're free from the blame and can find the bandwidth
to manage the current issues in your life."

Fort / If you were a handy child, you would know that building a
fortress is not as simple as tossing a blanket over two chairs or the back
of a couch—it's a feat of architecture and hoarding, finding the perfect
combination of blankets, pillows, movies, snacks, and lights to create
the ultimate cave that you can crawl into and become a hermit in until

you feel marginally better about the world that's waiting for you outside. You're never too old to create a safe space for yourself—and forts are particularly playful places that can help you feel protected and cozy.

Their Care: "Self-care, for me—a bipolar depressive with borderline personality disorder—is complicated. I am constantly chasing that rush of doing something for myself. 'This will make me happy,' I say. 'Yes, Sephora, I need that serum because then people will look at me and say, *Wow, her skin looks nice, I wish my life was as together as hers.*' I have a skin care collection that others dream of, every kind of bath product, books and films and movies stuffed into corners of my room like secrets.

"But it also means having no money. Ever. And there's always regret. Why do I always have to be the mess? Self-care is so essential, but my identity is too deeply tied to it. I'm still figuring out how to make self-care not hurt a little every time. It's a work in progress."

—Taylor, 28, Milwaukee, WI

Fresh Clothes / Even if you're not leaving the house, change into clean clothes. You'll feel a little more OK. They don't even have to be *real clothes*. PJs work just fine. There's no scientific proof out there that wrinkly or musty or lived-in clothes absorb your sadness, but shedding them is freeing, anyway.

Friends / So much can be said about the positive impact friends can have on our mental health and our lives in general. You might be tempted to sequester yourself away when you're going through something—which is understandable. A lot of us feel the need to put on our best face, even to our friends, or to not burden them with our problems. But so many negative emotions breed in isolation, and good friends will show up for you when you need a little care. So enjoy their company, lean on them, and appreciate the ways their presence is healing.

WHAT ABOUT NOT-SO-GOOD FRIENDS?

There's a lot of talk about toxic friends, but that can feel like an extremely low bar to set when it comes to evaluating your friendships and whether they're worth your time and energy. Toxic or not, here are some signs it might be time to make a change:

❖ You feel drained after hanging out with them.

❖ You don't like how you act when you're around them.

❖ You need to psyche yourself up to see them.

❖ The balance is way off. Either they don't reciprocate your effort or vice versa.

❖ They make you feel bad about yourself, pressure or guilt-trip you, or frequently fight with you.

❖ You just don't like or respect them anymore.

You'll have to evaluate for yourself which route is best, whether it's setting new boundaries for your friendship, phasing it out slowly, or formally ending it. Also important to recognize is that setting these boundaries and making these cuts are your responsibility. Like Oprah Winfrey said, "If friends disappoint you over and over, that's in large part your own fault. Once someone has shown a tendency to be self-centered, you need to recognize that and take care of yourself; people aren't going to change simply because you want them to."

Their Care: "My family has a history of mental illnesses that I wasn't made aware of until it directly affected me. My mother was diagnosed as clinically depressed two years ago, which caused me to (kind of) live alone for a whole year and a half.

"I, thankfully, had great people around me. I think it's important for ladies to have their gal friends. Their down-to-earth, weird, hilariously blunt, and accepting ladies. Girls support girls. People support people. Friends drag their friends out of the house and make the best memories out of spontaneous moments. Little things like getting coffee, running errands, spending waaaay too much money getting sushi every week, and, my personal favorite, the karaoke car ride. There is nothing better than a good old off-beat, off-key rendition of your favorite song with your best friends."

—Tina, 18, California

Friendship Bracelets / At a certain age, friendship bracelets stop being a *thing*, but oh my god, bring them back. The good old-fashioned friendship bracelet is the most underrated craft: It's repetitive, meditative, and incredibly soothing. Making these bracelets is relatively quick and easy for a satisfying jolt of productive energy and the rush of finishing something. Most importantly, when you're done, you have something to give to your friends. They might not wear it, but they'll treasure it lovingly.

Future You / It can be hard to consider Future Me. Present Me is *right here* and she has wants and needs and, frankly, is a lot more persuasive. Her voice is loud. But Present Me eventually becomes Future Me, and I will regret all the ways I'm not looking out for her. Many aspects of self-care are just little gifts to your future self: doing the dishes before you go to bed, filling up a water bottle and preparing hangover food before you go out for the night, exercising self-control over behaviors you know always make Future You ask, *Why did I do that?* These things are just ways of having empathy for your future self, and empathy is a muscle that gets stronger with every use.

> # Empathy is a muscle that gets stronger with every use.

Games / For the days when you know in theory that it might help to
be around people but you have the social energy of a depressed piece
of wallpaper, games are the answer. You don't have to worry about
being particularly charming or talkative; there are literally instructions
and maps for how you'll spend your evening, and focusing on the
rules or immersing yourself in the world of a game—whether it's an
intense RPG or Scrabble—gets you outside of your head. Set up a
regular game night with your friends if you tend to isolate yourself
and need some accountability.

Also, you know, games are fun. That's reason enough.

Gardening / The physical and mental benefits of getting fresh air speak for themselves, but many, many people find the act of taking care of plants—getting your hands dirty, tending to something so it can thrive, growing something simply because it's beautiful or nourishing—to be restorative and transformative. As the old saying goes, "To plant a garden is to believe in tomorrow."

Goal Audit / Goals are a big part of self-care because they represent what you want out of life—and a lot of unhappiness can stem from letting them go unrealized. But managing your goals is tricky. First, you have to make sure that you actually still *want* to accomplish all the goals you've set for yourself. You might realize you've been sticking with something out of obligation instead of actual desire. Like, it's OK if you don't actually want to run a 10K or write a book anymore, even if it's been on your bucket list since you were thirteen. Ditch the outdated goals hanging over you so they can stop causing you unneeded stress and guilt, and pick new ones that serve you now.

Once you have an updated list of goals you want to work toward, it's a good time to make sure those goals are specific and measurable. So, instead of ~publish a book~, start with "finish first draft by September," which is easier to make a game plan for. After that, check in with yourself regularly. Otherwise, your goals might remain these vague, far-off things that you'll get around to "one day" until you realize you never did. *See also* Prioritize.

Gratitude / Ask any number of therapists for their top piece of advice that anyone can do to improve their mental health, and I bet that a good percentage of them will tell you to practice gratitude. When you make a habit of noticing what you have, you eventually start to appreciate things a little more naturally, and that helps you feel measurably more content. Making gratitude a part of your life can mean updating a gratitude journal daily, jotting down a little gratitude list during a particularly low moment, tipping super generously, or writing a thank-you letter to someone you really appreciate. It might feel stupid at first, especially if you feel like your life is falling apart and giving you nothing to be grateful about, but try anyway. You might surprise yourself with what you start noticing.

MY GRATITUDE JOURNAL:

❋ I'm grateful for my cats' toe beans.

❋ I'm grateful I don't have allergies.

❋ I'm grateful that all of *Boy Meets World* is on Hulu.

❋ I'm grateful for the candle aisle at TJ Maxx.

❋ I'm grateful for my internet connection.

❋ I'm grateful for Wellbutrin and Prozac.

❋ I'm grateful that you're reading these words right now, what the fuck????

GET SWEPT UP
IN A FRUITFUL
SEARCH FOR
REASONS TO SAY
"THANK YOU."
—JOHN M. GOTTMAN

Habits / Remember that arsenal of fortifying habits we talked about? Good self-care isn't something you do just once—you have to commit to doing the things you know make you feel better regularly, not only damage control.

Sadly, when it comes to forming healthy habits, there's no one-size-fits-all formula to making them stick. You've probably heard about various secrets that promise to finally help you form that habit. Just do it for thirty days, and it will stick! Schedule in a cheat day! Do it first thing in the morning! Et cetera, et cetera, et cetera. Those methods are effective for some people, but not for everyone. The important point is to find out what works for you.

One thing that can help is asking yourself: *When was the last time I met a goal that I set for myself, stuck to a hobby or habit, or finished a project? What do I think led to my success?* For example, maybe the last time you were able to paint consistently was in college—and it was probably because you had a structured environment keeping you accountable. Or maybe you started working out three times a week only when your brother said there was no way you could ever do more push-ups than him—and you needed to prove him wrong.

What you *might* discover is that you react positively or negatively to different kinds of expectations, specifically outer expectations (such as deadlines, assignments, pressure from friends) or inner expectations (things you do for yourself for personal reasons). According to Gretchen Rubin, happiness expert and author of *The Four Tendencies*, there tend to be four kinds of people:

- **UPHOLDERS:** those who respond well to both inner and outer expectations.
- **QUESTIONERS:** those who question outer expectations but can fulfill their inner expectations for themselves.
- **OBLIGERS:** those who meet outer expectations but have a hard time meeting expectations they impose on themselves.
- **REBELS:** those who resist all expectations, inner and outer, and need freedom.

Once you have an idea of which of the four camps you fall into, you have a better chance at setting yourself up for success. For example, once you accept that you have a hard time self-motivating, that could be a sign that you need to come up with a system of accountability to keep you motivated as you try to develop a desired habit.

Their Care: "Last summer, I was hospitalized for depression, and the experience was incredibly transformative and healing. When I entered hospital treatment I was at a point where I really hated the phrase 'self-care.' I felt betrayed by the popular conception of self-care as this kind of forgiving world where indulging my every impulse was a good thing. Because I'd tried that, and shockingly, it had not made me feel better. Like, I was very depressed, so I would buy myself a scented candle. But then I was just a very depressed person with a scented candle. Which kind of takes the fun out of scented candles.

"But during my hospital treatment, I had to grow up and come to terms with the fact that self-care is about making wise choices and thoughtful, intentional decisions: *Will this make me feel better right now? Will this make me feel better in the long term? Or, bare minimum, will it not make me feel worse?* Sometimes that means things that are fun, like candles, and sometimes it means things that are hard, like sending emails about student loans. Caring for yourself is like caring for anyone or anything else—there are rewarding parts and exhausting parts. Self-care is about giving myself tools for tolerance. Self-care is fortifying. It's strengthening. I used to think it was about giving yourself what you want, but at best that's a happy side effect: Self-care is giving yourself what you need."

—Sophie, 19, San Francisco, CA

Heat / For anyone who deals with chronic pain, and anyone who has been injured, heat therapy often finds its way into their healing regimen. That's because applying heat to an area improves circulation and promotes recovery—plus, it loosens muscles, which contributes to pain relief. It can also just feel really, really nice. Stock up on all the heated amenities—pads, mattress toppers, jackets, car seats, hot-water bottles, whatever. You can soothe your aches and pains if you have them, or you can simply enjoy the warmth and coziness.

Horror Movies / For some people, particularly people dealing
with anxiety, PTSD, and disassociation, horror movies provide a way
to be scared in a controlled environment. If your brain and body
work against you in the form of panic attacks, flashbacks, dissociative
episodes, obsessive thoughts, *whatever*, then having control over
what's triggering physiological responses—increased heartbeat, rapid
breathing, or even just general fear—through watching a scary movie
can, in a weird way, be soothing and help you feel more grounded in
your body.

Hotel / Believe me when I say I know how bougie it sounds when I
suggest treating yourself to a rejuvenating stay in a hotel. But if you
know where to look, you can book yourself a room so cheap you'll
feel like you got away with the scam of the year. I don't do it often,
but when I do, it's usually in one of two circumstances: when I need
a bath, because I certainly don't have one in my Brooklyn apartment,
and when said apartment has turned into a messy depression den
that's stressing me out and I still don't have the bandwidth to clean it.
So I go on Hotel Tonight or Extreme
Hotel Deals and drop fifty dollars to
have a place to escape to. It's still an
investment, but you know in your gut
when the luxury is worth the cost, and
damn it, sometimes it is.

Hydrate / Water, water, water, water,
water. Even at rock bottom, you will
feel a tiny bit better if you're not also

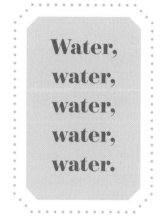

**Water,
water,
water,
water,
water.**

dehydrated. There are a lot of apps out there that remind you to drink and even high-tech water bottles that signal when it's time to take a sip. Thanks, technology.

Hygge / Hygge (pronounced *hue-guh*) is a Danish concept that has

infiltrated the lifestyle and wellness spheres in recent years. There's no direct translation to English, but hygge encompasses a feeling of coziness and contentment. Think: enjoying a cup of tea during a rainy day or relaxing by the fire in the winter or decorating your space with soft throw pillows and blankets.

In *The Little Book of Hygge*, Meik Wiking, the CEO of the Happiness Research Institute in Copenhagen, describes hygge as "a defining feature of our cultural identity and an integral part of the national DNA," which may be why Denmark is consistently at the top of the list of the world's happiest countries. If you're already a fan of coziness, it couldn't hurt to try really leaning into this whole hygge thing as a deliberate lifestyle. Curate your candle collection, pick a day of the week to indulge in your favorite comfort food, and commit to infusing your life with the things that make you feel safe and warm.

Hygiene / Good hygiene tends to be one of the

first things to go when life gets rough, and it's also one that can make you feel a bit more human when you do actually practice it. So check in with yourself: Have you brushed your teeth or showered lately? Try that first, and be gentle with yourself if you have to take it slow.

Identify Problems / A CBT technique to counteract negative thoughts—remember those cognitive distortions—is identifying problems and brainstorming solutions rather than ruminating. You don't even have to plan on following through, though of course it's great if you do. But since we're wired to feel helpless and hopeless when we're depressed, even writing a list of little things you can do to problem-solve can ease those feelings.

Imagery-Based Exposure / This may seem

counterintuitive, since dwelling on the past is typically *bad* for depression and anxiety, but done correctly, spending time thinking about memories that trigger strong emotions lessens their impact. Visualize a negative situation and analyze it in detail, by remembering both what happened *and* what emotions and thoughts you had during the experience. Exposing yourself to a bad memory over and over can take away some of its power to trigger you or even desensitize you to it until you're like, "Humiliating public gaffe, whomst?"

Indulge / Indulging as a means of self-care isn't really about blowing

your money on something expensive or otherwise numbing your feelings through consumption; it's more about allowing yourself to feel true, genuine pleasure in a given moment. (It's hard not to be present when you're eating the fancy chocolate or snuggling in a really wonderful set of sheets, y'know?)

Their Care: "Self-care can definitely be in the form of a treat, like a special dessert, a fancy candle, etc. on some occasions, but I think it's important to remember that companies trying to sell 'self-care items' are not doing it for caring, but for profit. Taking care of yourself needs to start with a good self-awareness of your own needs. If, for instance, you find yourself constantly reaching for 'stress-relief self-care treats,' after a while, true self-care needs to be an assessment of why you feel so stressed all the time and what can be done to mitigate that, not another essential oil shopping spree."

—**Kate, 29, Falls Church, VA**

Intentions / I'll be honest—it took me a while to come around to setting intentions. The way I imagined intentions—as life mottoes like "find balance" and "live with love"—felt too intangible, too impractical, too incompatible with the deliberate way I live my life. I thought of setting intentions as nothing more than weightless wishes you put into the universe in hopes that everything you want will waft your way simply because you spoke them into existence.

But frankly, I was really underestimating what intentions have the power to be. And you might be, too. Setting intentions boils down to one thing: a plan where you might otherwise operate on autopilot. Intentions give you a way to focus on who you want to be and what you want to do, and they help you create a roadmap for getting there. Otherwise, it's so easy to just . . . not.

Because here's the thing about taking a moment to think intentionally about guiding principles for your life: It makes a huge difference in helping you create the life you want!!! Shocking, I know. It's about taking the time to say, *This is my purpose, this is the energy that will carry me, this is what I'm going to concentrate on, this is how I want to live.*

Once you know these things, it's wild how other things—like what to say yes and no to, or which parts of your life to change or nourish—just become so much easier.

> **Intentions really boil down to one thing: make a plan where you might otherwise operate on autopilot.**

Internet Friends / You may wonder

why internet friends aren't included under the Friends entry. It's not because I don't think internet friends can be as good as IRL friends. It's actually the opposite: I believe that internet friends deserve their own special shout-out because too many people think that their internet friends don't count.

Like, sure, it might not be traditional and it's hard to shake years of hiding your internet friends from your guardians because of their internalized sense of stranger danger. (I know I'm not the only one who has explained away online friends with flimsy excuses like, "Oh yeah, she went to my school, but then she moved and now she lives in London!")

But my question is, why wouldn't you treat yourself to making some friends on the internet? It's a portal that streamlines the search for humans you have a lot in common with. Plus, it's great if you have a hard time making friends IRL for whatever reason, such as social anxiety, mobility issues, or insecurity. At this point, everyone should have internet friends—we spend too much time online not to.

> No matter how lonely and isolated
> and starved for connection you are,
> there's always the possibility in
> the online world that you can find
> a place to be accepted, or discover
> a friendship that's started with the
> smallest of interests but could last
> a lifetime. —**Felicia Day**

Intuition / Trusting your gut—or even interpreting what your gut is trying to tell you—is *not* easy. Especially if your brain is also home to anxiety and intrusive thoughts and years of defense mechanisms developed in the face of trauma. But the only place to start is to tune in to your internal compass and listen. The more you learn to identify when your instincts are trying to communicate with you, the more you can eventually learn to trust them. And the more you can trust your instincts, the more confidently you can act in your own best interest and well-being—even if that means making difficult choices.

Joke / Sometimes all you can do is make light of the shit you're going through, because when you treat things as less serious, they can *feel* less serious. For an article in *The Atlantic*, writer Elizabeth Anne Brown talked to suicide experts about how the genre of dark memes popping up on Twitter and Instagram might actually be therapeutic. She writes, "Typically, suicide memers aren't mocking suicidal thoughts; they're commiserating and bonding over being suicidal. Morbid memes, these experts believe, may be a foot in the door to one of the most vulnerable and hard-to-reach populations: socially isolated young people."

So hey, if it works for you, find some way-too-relatable memes or crack a few darkly funny or self-deprecating jokes.

> **Sometimes all you can do is make light of the shit you're going through, because when you treat things as less serious, they can *feel* less serious.**

Journal / Not only is it satisfying as hell to get all your emotions out on paper, but expressive and reflective writing has also been shown to help your mental well-being. If you don't journal regularly, it can be hard to know where to start. Journaling doesn't have to be anything more complicated than talking about your day, your emotions, or things you're excited or frustrated about. But if you want to go beyond that, or if you're stuck, a quick Google search for journal prompts will give you a lot to work with.

One caveat about journaling, though: There's a line between beneficial and harmful rumination. If you're someone who feels the need to write at length about your negative emotions and experiences and find yourself obsessing, it might not be the best tool for you. If you're worried about that but still want to write, limit yourself to one page at a time. Or instead of writing detailed passages, try expressing yourself in a less literal way, like journaling in verse and poetry.

Journaling can help you reflect on positive things when you're feeling really down. Here are some ideas to get you started:

❋ What's your favorite childhood memory?

❋ What's the nicest thing someone has ever done for you?

❋ What's the nicest thing you've ever done for someone else?

❋ Who was your role model growing up?

❋ What is your biggest dream in life?

❋ What would your perfect day look like?

❋ What makes you unique?

❋ How would your best friend describe you?

❋ What things are you most grateful for?

Knit / As writer Alanna Okun puts it in an essay for BuzzFeed, knitting dims the roar—of anxiety, of sadness, of anger, of any unsavory feeling that needs smoothing over. She writes, "Crafting is a lot like sex or yoga, how it shrinks your immediate world down to this cozy, manageable size where all you have to focus on is what's right in front of you; unlike sex, at the end you get a new pair of socks or a coaster."

Their Care: "I'm an artist who used to make things full time in a studio outside my home. For the past eight months, since my father's death, I've been a full-time caregiver for my disabled elderly mother who does not have dementia but who suffers with lifelong depression and anxiety. My husband and I moved into her home basically overnight so she can continue to live here. My husband and I are living in my childhood bedroom and I have taken over for my mom as property manager, chief financial officer, cook, cleaner, cheerleader, and all-around assistant.

"When people hear of my circumstances they always say, with a lot of compassion, 'Don't forget to do self-care' which is unintentionally extremely irritating because of course I will do whatever I can to make things better for myself, but the overall situation is inherently tragic and my life is no longer my own for who knows how many more years. A hot bath won't fix that.

"To me, self-care means making the best of a bad moment in the moment, over and over. It means letting myself waste time. I like to buy too much fabric and quilting magazines to make small crafts either to keep, sell, or send people as gifts."

—Liz, 49, Lowell, MA

Know Yourself / So much of taking care of yourself is rooted in actually knowing yourself and your needs. Even Socrates was like, "know thyself, for once we know ourselves, we may learn how to care for ourselves." Classical Greek self-care, anyone? Make a concerted effort to observe yourself—your habits, your patterns, your tics, your vulnerabilities. Find unique ways to get to know yourself, such as by going to therapy, journaling, or taking a solo trip. Gathering this info over time will turn you into an expert on your needs.

SO MUCH OF
TAKING CARE
OF YOURSELF
IS ROOTED
IN ACTUALLY
KNOWING
YOURSELF AND
YOUR NEEDS.

Laugh / OK, do something for me right now. You might feel a little stupid, but just trust me. Make yourself laugh. Literally. Start with one (HA!), then two (HA HA!), then three (HA HA HA!) and so on and so forth. I have *never* made it to the seventh HA! without finding myself genuinely cracking up. Is it silly? Yes. But that's the point; sometimes you need silly.

START WITH ONE
(HA!),
THEN TWO
(HA HA!),
THEN THREE
(HA HA HA!)

L

Leave Situations / We often forget this is an option. Like when you're feeling anxious at a party, rooted to the ground beside the snack table. Or when you drag yourself out of the house when you're depressed only to realize that your original instinct was on the money: you don't have the bandwidth to be around people. When you're uncomfortable or a situation is exacerbating feelings of sadness, anxiety, loneliness, or anger, it's OK to just . . . leave. Even if it's just to step outside for a little air.

Let Go / We all have things we hold on to longer than we should: memories, people, grudges, embarrassments, goals, and personas that we've let overstay their welcome because it feels safer than letting them go and finding out what's left. Even old pains and resentments are comforting in their familiarity, less risky than the unknown. But when we make the mistake of holding on to them too tightly, they seep under our skin and become part of our identities.

What are you holding on to that is no longer serving you? Let go of names that still make your hackles rise and draw unkind words to your lips. Let go of memories that curdle your blood and drag you back to the past. Let go of old goals that fill you with dread more than excitement. Let go of the victories you've been resting on for so long you've forgotten how to take a step forward. Take stock of those thoughts that you push to the back of your mind because they make you mad just thinking about them. At some point you'll realize that these things you've been hoarding—figuratively and literally—have left no room for the new. Don't let your heart and your life become repositories for ancient history.

Let It Out / It can be so satisfying to release your emotions

instead of sitting quietly with them swirling inside. And while you can't always yell your rage from the rooftops or hurl your sadness off a mountain, you can probably find a decent outlet that gives you the same satisfaction. Allow yourself a hearty cry. Take a kickboxing class. Create a messy work of art.

Their Care: "I'm trying to relearn how to love my body. It's hard. When I was twenty-five I got diagnosed with thyroid cancer and they had to take my thyroid out—I ended up gaining forty pounds in six weeks and had to throw out all of my clothes. I'm still tired all of the time; sometimes I actually cry just thinking back at how active and vibrant I used to be. So, my self-care is all about coming to terms with my new body, whatever that means.

"To be honest, the most liberating thing is just saying, 'Fuck it!' and screaming into the social media void about how angry I am. Just talking about how much I resent my body and how I don't want to love it anymore makes me feel like I went through something real. It's so . . . messy. And emotional. And raw. But I love being a goddamn angry woman. And it's giving me the confidence to dress how I want and walk around in public without hating myself all of the time."

—Jessica, 28, Bloomington, IN

Lists / Making lists is an easy grounding exercise that only requires a pen and paper, or even just the notes app on your phone. You can make lists of anything: states, names, colors, movies, songs. Pick a theme and jot down as many words as you can. Though coming up with items to put on the list is pretty simple, it requires your full attention, making it the perfect activity to zone in on while waiting for anxiety to pass.

Listen / There is so much noise in the world. Music, nature, people, impact, movement. All the weird, nebulous sounds that are so satisfying for some reason—a baby laughing, a can of soda opening, heels clicking on a hardwood floor. A cork popping. The right song can sink under your skin and dance through your bloodstream. An unexpected murmur can send static from your scalp down your spine. But how often do you really listen? Try tuning in. There's a difference been hearing and listening, after all. Hearing is passive, noises wafting up against your attention. Listening, though, is active. Making time for it might involve slowing down a little bit, but that's not a bad thing, is it?

Put on your headphones, close your eyes, and let your favorite song wash over you, or play through an album from start to finish. Bonus points if you do it in the dark. Go outside and identify all the sounds you can—wildlife, the rustling of leaves, the crunch of gravel underfoot. Let a good lecture get its hooks into your brain and imprint on your memory. Fall down a YouTube rabbit hole and see if you can find an autonomous sensory meridian response (ASMR) video that triggers those elusive tingles.

Their Care: "I am a female liberal conservationist living in Trump's America and working at a job that frustrates and belittles me, and so I am always needing to create a protective bubble around myself when I am overwhelmed by the badness all around, and the badness from within. My first healthy step is finding music that always lifts my spirits. If I can sing along to music that also lifts my spirits, that is a huge help."

—Karina, 49, San Diego, CA

Little Acts of Kindness / Sometimes caring for other people is a roundabout way of caring for yourself and that's OK. Good deeds don't need to be 100 percent selfless. Making other people happy—whether it's loved ones or strangers—has the power to get you out of your own head and give you a small sense of purpose, even when you're feeling the most down and useless.

WHAT DOES AN ACT OF KINDNESS ACTUALLY LOOK LIKE?

✳ Run an errand for a friend who is totally swamped.

✳ Offer to babysit or pet sit for someone who needs a night off or a weekend out of town.

✳ Randomly text your friends your favorite things about them or memories you cherish.

✳ Look into volunteering opportunities in your area.

✳ Call a loved one you don't talk to often but who you know would love to hear from you.

✳ Have coffee with that recent grad who wants to "pick your brain" about what you do.

✳ Ask your coworkers if you can grab them anything on your coffee run—you don't need to foot the bill; spending the time and energy is kindness enough.

WITH A LITTLE CREATIVE THINKING, YOU CAN HACK THE WAYS YOUR MENTAL HEALTH DISRUPTS YOUR LIFE.

Lounge in Something Comfy / I'm a big fan of

intentional lounging, especially when it's done wearing something clean and cozy that feels *slightly* more elevated than your mismatched, grungy Sunday outfit. (Think: matching jammies, a fluffy robe, the perfect hoodie, and basketball pants. If nothing else, at least aim for putting on a clean pair of underwear.) The clothes we wear matter and can have a big effect on our overall mood; it's worth it to put on clothes that make you feel better, not worse. *See also* Hygge.

Loopholes / Do you have obsessive thoughts about having left

your straightening iron on that distract you during work? Just take it with you when you leave the house. Does having to do dishes make you reluctant to cook? Buy paper plates. Do body image issues get in the way of hygiene because you don't like to see yourself naked? Shower in the dark. With a little creative thinking, you can probably hack the ways your mental health disrupts your life—they may not be conventional solutions, but if they work, they work.

Maintain / Sometimes, maintenance is all you can—and should—go for.

We live in a society obsessed with self-improvement. We're constantly told that we should be doing better, achieving more, making changes. That's not only deeply annoying, it's fundamentally unreasonable. But even if we know, rationally, that no one is always moving upward and onward, the idea that we *should* be can be especially discouraging when we're going through a hard time or dealing with any sort of illness, mental or physical.

Maintenance takes work and is also deeply helpful. Give yourself permission to concentrate on that, without guilting yourself about other things you think you should be doing. Maintain your good coping mechanisms. Maintain going to therapy and taking your medication. Maintain doing *just OK* if doing *great* isn't in your reach.

Maintenance takes work.

Their Care: "I always have to be aware of my body in a way that other people don't have to be. I don't have a functioning pituitary gland, which doctors sometimes call the 'master gland' because it's in charge of so many things. What this means practically is that I have to manually introduce and regulate all the hormones that naturally fluctuate throughout the day for everyone else.

"Have you ever thought about thirst? Like, actually thought about that feeling? Probably not! And that's OK! You feel thirsty, you drink something, you don't feel thirsty anymore. That cycle is innate, and is triggered by a hormone my body doesn't make. So I take a pill three times a day to keep that cycle from spiraling into what my mom calls the unquenchable thirsties. At that point, no matter how much water I drink, I still feel like I've been in the Sahara for two weeks without water. I can drink until I vomit from fullness and still feel parched. I can give myself water poisoning! I always have to be checking in with my body to decide when to take my afternoon dose of medication to keep that spiral at bay.

"Is this self-care? The term has become so corrupted by the idea of ~relaxation~ that it almost feels dismissive to call monitoring and maintaining my health self-care and not just . . . my life."

—Nikki, 26, Seattle, WA

Make Your Bed / It's one of the simplest things you can do to

feel a little bit more OK and in control. Retired United States Navy officer William H. McRaven once said in a commencement speech at the University of Texas that if you want to change the world, you should start by making your bed.

"If you make your bed every morning, you will have accomplished the first task of the day," he advised.
"It will give you a small sense of pride, and it will encourage you to do another task, and another, and another. And by the end of the day that one task completed will have turned into many tasks completed."

And also, is there anything more satisfying than crawling into a made bed at the end of a long day?

Manage Your Expectations / I don't mean be

pessimistic—just be mindful that your expectations aren't unrealistic. There will be good days and bad days, positive outcomes and negative outcomes. And as empowerment coach Christine Hassler writes in her book *Expectation Hangover*, the expectation that we should be happy all the time or always get our way pretty much guarantees letdown. There's looking on the bright side, and then there's just setting yourself up for disappointment.

Medication / Medication isn't for everyone, but it's a totally viable option to talk about with your doctor if you're dealing with any number of health struggles. And keeping up on those medications is self-care. Do what you need to do to make sure you don't forget to take your meds. Get a cute pillbox, keep a water bottle next to your bed, set an alarm.

Meditate / Meditation is one of those things that you kind of just have to say "Sounds fake, but OK" to, and then give it a try (start with just three to five minutes) with a super open mind and basically no expectations. There are apps out there like Calm and Headspace that can guide you.

But if that's really not for you, by definition, meditation—using a technique, *any* technique, to train your attention and awareness—can be practiced a million different ways. Yes, most often it's a mindfulness practice or a focused thought exercise, but that's only the start. Any task where you need to pay full attention can be meditative, like riding a motorcycle or playing a complicated game.

Meet Yourself Where You're At / With all these

messages about what self-care should look like, it's really discouraging when so much of it feels out of your reach. Self-care is a skill—and like any skill, it requires practice. If this is your first time prioritizing taking care of yourself as part of your daily routine, it could be anything from awkward to *actually difficult*. That's OK—self-care exists on a spectrum and the important thing is to be gentle with yourself and meet yourself where you're at. There will be setbacks, days or weeks or even months when you feel like you're backsliding. The most you can do is try your best, and when I say *try your best*, I mean acknowledge that on some days your best won't be very good. It happens.

> ## Self-care is a skill—and like any skill, it requires practice.

Their Care: "My self-care skills are poor. There is a big traumatic thing that has happened to me, and it affects me daily. I've had no choice but to cut my hair off twice now because of me simply not brushing it. I peel the skin around my fingers off and they scar. I often can't practice self-care the way I want to, but I try to do smaller things like shave, lotion, use my favorite perfume."

—Abigail, 19, New Jersey

Mental Health Days / Sometimes you wake up and need

a mental health day without notice. Other times you'll be able to anticipate when you'll need time to recover. For example, you might take an extra day after a weekend with your stressful AF parents or call out from work the day of a therapy appointment when you know you're *really* going to get into some shit.

The thing is, if I took a mental health day every time my depression or anxiety was flaring up, there would be weeklong stretches where I didn't go to work. So you have to be smart about them. First of all, don't make mental health days your go-to solution. On days that you wake up and aren't feeling great mentally, go in, but give yourself permission to leave early if you don't improve—chances are pretty high that you'll feel better once you get to work or school.

When you *do* take them, mental health days are great in theory, but most people don't use them effectively—we spend them sleeping, watching Netflix, or doing nothing at all. *I know that's tempting*, but according to therapists, you'll feel much better if you plan out what you'll do when you take them. A good mental health day should be action- or task-filled, because you feel better when you're productive and living with purpose. For example, if you're taking a day because you really hate your job and it's making you miserable, use the day to meet with a career coach and apply for new jobs. Or if that's just not in your bandwidth (understandable), work on low-energy activities you enjoy.

Of course, it's about listening to your body, too. We all need a blanket burrito day every once in a while, so don't push yourself if you really just need time to catch up on sleep, relieve pain, or do nothing at all.

Mirror / Sometimes it's easier to pick up new habits and attitudes when you have a good role model to follow, so choose someone you admire in a way you want to emulate and let them be your guide. Whether that's a historical figure, a fictional one, a celebrity, a family member, or a friend, you can tap into how they have inspired you and use their energy in a healing or guiding way. Don't be creepy about it, but observe what you can learn from them. How do they accomplish what they accomplish? *Why* are they so lovely to be around? How do they manage their overflowing schedules?

Move / The frustrating thing about exercise is that it's both incredibly good for your mental health and incredibly difficult to do when your mental health is suffering. You'll have to find what works for you—it might be as small as taking a regular trip around the block—but it's worth it once you do.

Their Care: "I'm Puerto Rican and from the Bronx, have been in therapy for one year, and am seeing a nurse practitioner for the first time to consider medication. I come from a low-income household that, unfortunately like many Puerto Rican families, doesn't believe in psychology. No one in my family has sought treatment and they do not encourage looking. Self-care for me right now is going to a barre class once a week. For a long time I had an eating disorder and the exercise makes it easier to feel 'OK' about what I eat daily. It's the bougiest thing in the world and everyone in the room with me is white, hates talking, and is intense, but it's one of the few coping mechanisms that has worked."

—Audrey, 27, New York City

IN CASE YOU NEED IT, HERE ARE SOME NOT-OVERWHELMING TIPS TO MOVE YOUR BODY WHEN IT'S HARD:

- Try a short workout app or video to get a quick workout that doesn't require you to leave your bedroom.

- Write a letter to yourself as a reminder that you'll feel good after you sweat a little.

- Start your day off by stretching in bed.

- Carry around your workout gear just in case, because you never know when the rare mood will strike.

- Exercise at home where you won't feel watched or judged.

- Don't put pressure on yourself to complete a whole program or stick to a strict schedule.

- Make your after-workout shower super luxurious so you have something to look forward to.

- Integrate exercise into your day in non-negotiable ways, like biking to work.

- Consider renting equipment for a more accessible alternative to the gym.

- Dance around your room to pump-up music. Seriously. It might not be the gym, but it still gets your heart pumping and does a lot to wake up your soul.

- Trust that your body will eventually get on board with your routine—and you might even wind up liking it. And if you don't, you can always try something new.

- Above all, be kind to yourself and accept that some days it's not going to happen—and that's OK.

Moderation /

You knew this had to be in here. Anything in this book can be bad for you if you don't exercise it in moderation. There are also certain self-care habits that will inevitably lead to a point of diminishing returns. You have to save some things for special occasions if you actually want them to feel special.

Additionally, you have to leave yourself slack for when you mess up. Even with the habits that *wouldn't* be bad to stick to every day (such as setting good boundaries, calling your mom, or drinking eight glasses of water), you're going to mess up. And that's fine.

Their Care: "I am so frustrated by the recent surge in consumerist self-care products. Wellness isn't a product. For me, self-care is holding myself accountable in my daily habits to build better health and well-being. I put strict limits on alcohol and retail therapy so that through enforcing compassionate self-discipline I can mitigate my lethargy and function well, even when my depression and executive dysfunction are bad. It's about staying one step ahead of the disarray and neglect that my mental illness leaves me vulnerable to."

—Riv, 31, Portland, OR

YOU HAVE TO SAVE SOME THINGS FOR SPECIAL OCCASIONS IF YOU ACTUALLY WANT THEM TO FEEL SPECIAL.

Name What's Upsetting You / We've all been

there: Some straw breaks the metaphorical camel's back of your
emotions and you have a strong reaction to a small argument,
misunderstanding, hiccup, or whatever. Get in the practice of
reflecting on what's really making you feel like shit—is there
something else going on that needs to be addressed and soothed?

Name Your Negative Voice / We've already established

that your inner voice can be a bitch and a liar and that you shouldn't
automatically believe that something is true just because you think it.

Another great way of battling your negative inner voice is to name it so that you can call it directly on its bullshit. Think of it as a separate person—yes, they're *your* negative thoughts, but there's no point in beating *yourself* up.

For example, if you want to name your negative voice Donald, think of Donald as a really annoying loudmouth backseat driver with no common sense or right to be passing judgment. This makes it much easier to shut the voice down.

You're going to fail this test. Shut up, Donald!

You suck and your friends hate you. Whatever you say, Donald!

Why bother with that dating app? You're going to die alone. LOL, you don't know what you're talking about, Donald!

Nature / Nature nurtures, and connecting with it can be incredibly healing. (Also, the sheer vastness of nature often helps put our own problems in perspective.) There are so many ways to let the earth take care of you. Get a little sunshine, breathe fresh air, spend some time near water, visit a public garden, read under a tree, feel the grass or sand beneath your feet, learn about octopuses or other cool animals, visit a natural history museum, study the moon . . . the list goes on and on.

LET THE EARTH
TAKE CARE
OF YOU.

Nest / Everyone needs a place where they can be wholly themselves. The world demands a lot of us: It asks us to put on masks, to smile when we have every reason not to, to make pleasantries, to keep certain things private, to adopt personas, to be uncomfortable. And honestly, abiding by the unspoken rules of existing as a person day in and day out can be exhausting. In order for it not to wear us down, we need somewhere we know we can peel off our layers after a long day of fulfilling expectations—a refuge where we can exist only for ourselves and no one else.

Take steps to create a place that is full of things you love, a pocket of the universe that is just for you. For some people, that's home, but not for everyone, so be creative if you have to. Infuse your surroundings with trinkets and tools that nourish and energize you. Stock your fridge with food for your favorite recipes. Frame photos of your people. Design the perfect reading nook. Hang lights that fill you with warmth. Find art that is incredibly *you*. When we take who we are and what we love and manifest it in a physical way—the colors of our spirit, the smells that remind us of our best memories, the textures that make us feel comforted and safe—we will always have a place where we belong.

You can start small, too. Make your bed the coziest place on earth. Decorate your desk so it's unmistakably yours. Make your room a calming oasis in a chaotic house. Build a shelf to hold your favorite things so you'll always have somewhere to look to feel at home. Find the corners of your life that you can transform little by little to reflect your heart and fulfill its needs.

Their Care: "I am the kind of person who is very goofy and fun in social situations but pretty neurotic and anxious behind the scenes. Nobody really knows because I never talk about it (and am deeply embarrassed about it), but I have a history with anorexia and disordered eating and being kind of manic about numbers—step counts, calories, word counts, page views—that in some ways has contributed a lot to my success as a writer. I have good friends and come from a nice family and although I am not the smartest or the funniest person in the room, I work really, really hard.

"To me self-care is mostly just being alone and not having to 'perform' for anybody. It's keeping my space clean so I can come home and write or read or just be on the internet. My day of the week is Saturday; I get up very early and go grocery shopping, then on a long run, then shower and let my hair air dry for once, then make myself the same large and elaborate brunch while I watch Netflix, then write for a bit, nap, write for a bit, go on a walk, and then come home and have wine with a lit Bath & Body Works candle before dinner. I look forward to this day all week—it's my reset button."

—**Summer, 27, New York City**

News Boundaries / Pretty much the easiest way to stress

yourself out right now is keeping up-to-date on everything that's
happening in the world. Yes, being informed is important, and
unplugging from the news for even a few hours at a time can feel like
burying your head in the sand, but it's crucial to set up some rules so
you're not constantly exposed to bad, stressful, and even potentially
traumatic news. What works and is actually realistic will be different
for everyone, but here are a few ways to think about it:

- **SET A TIME BOUNDARY.** Limit yourself to certain times throughout the day (like a half hour in the morning and half of your lunch break, for example) so you don't fall into a vortex of endless scrolling.

- **MAKE CERTAIN PLACES OFF-LIMITS TO NEWS.** Places like your bed or your workplace should be off-limits—just to create safe spaces to unplug.

- **READ ONLY HEADLINES UNTIL A PREAPPROVED TIME.** Skim news throughout the day so you don't feel completely disconnected, but save details for later.

- **CATCH UP ON THE NEWS AT THE END OF THE DAY.** To avoid getting sucked into a rabbit hole of news right before bed, sign up for an evening digest and limit yourself to that. Tons of news outlets have them, highlighting the most notable events that happened that day.

No / Say it more. Say it without apologizing. Say it because one of two

things inevitably happens when you say "yes" when you want to say
"no"—either you consent at the expense of your own well-being, or
you make excuses and flake later at the expense of your relationships.
Don't do that. Be gracious and polite, sure, but look out for yourself.

SAY IT MORE.
SAY IT WITHOUT
APOLOGIZING.
NO!

Online Shopping / Whenever the seasons are turning—
summer chilling into fall and fall freezing into winter until it all
inevitably melts again—I'm overcome with dread, and I can't be the
only one. Changing seasons means changing wardrobes and changing
wardrobes means shopping. I have dragged certain fall boots and
winter coats and summer dresses through the years in an iron grip to
avoid shopping. Why? Fitting rooms.

Fitting rooms, for anyone who has even a slightly complicated
relationship with their body, hold the potential to be another
dimension of hell. The fluorescent lighting, full-length mirrors, and

cramped space come together to put you on display like an art gallery of your biggest insecurities. It's the urban equivalent of *Naked and Afraid*.

Without fail, shopping ends, at best, in a huge plummet of mood and, at worst, in tears. And for this, online shopping is a savior. You'll want to make sure that where you shop has a simple and easy return policy, because it's true you won't get everything right the first time. But once you find stores and brands that you like, you'll develop a good sense of sizing and fit. Take a preventive strike against crying in a fitting room by tending to such a vulnerable errand in private.

Organize / Here's the thing: Being disorganized—and the feelings of being anxious, embarrassed, and flustered that come with it—typically doesn't feel *great*. It's also pretty hard to take care of yourself if you can't, say, get your prescription refilled. So investing some time and energy in organization is a really good way to feel a little bit better in the long run. *See also* Declutter.

Own Your Mistakes / Part of looking after yourself is knowing when you need to learn to do better. Not only will this help keep your relationships solid, but it'll keep at bay the 3 AM anxiety spirals about how you fucked up. This means swallow your pride and apologize, admit, and acknowledge.

DON'T KNOW WHERE TO BEGIN? HERE ARE SOME TIPS TO HELP YOU GET ORGANIZED:

- Organization looks different for everyone, but the bottom line is making sure everything has its place. That counts for both the tangible (like what dishes go where in your kitchen cabinets) and the intangible (like where you keep track of upcoming appointments).

- Take it one project at a time. Deciding you're going to organize your entire life is admirable and all, but it's also a recipe for disaster and burnout. You don't necessarily need to start small, but you can. Personally, I tackle my organization projects in order of urgency. Yes, my junk drawer might be easier to handle, but it's my unruly closet that brings me the most angst.

- It's a lot easier to organize if you have less junk, so you might want to start with paring down your belongings.

Pamper / They may *way* oversimplify the concept of self-care, but sheet masks and bath bombs became the misguided face of the self-care movement for a reason. Spoiling yourself feels *good*. It's relaxing and comes with a glow.

If you're not into that kind of thing, you can make up your own definition of pampering. It just means indulging yourself with attention and comfort in some way. Get a massage, enjoy a fancy meal, get your hair done before a big event or just because, or clear your weekend of plans so you can sleep in as long as you want.

Their Care: "I am a female business owner, which means I get a lot of gender-based oppression *every damn day*. I also have bipolar and anxiety disorders and suffer from suicidal ideation. If I don't practice my self-care, I lose control of everything else.

"My go-to self-care are my weekend rituals: face mask, bubble bath, exfoliating, clipping my cuticles, painting my nails, scrubbing my scalp, masturbation, and at least five or six hours sitting in front of the TV (an indulgence I rarely allow myself on weekdays) to decompress. When I do a big bubble bath, I have all types of exfoliants on hand because I feel like once a week, especially living in NYC and of course during the winter, I really need to scrub myself down. I'm not sure if it's metaphorical, but I always feel like I'm scrubbing the week away.

"Sometimes, I think, *Well, I'm just so tired, I'll take a quick shower and then be done with it*, but that doesn't give me the same space to check in with myself, take stock of my needs and emotions. If I skip my ritual once, it may take weeks before I get back on my routines that are essential for me to function with my mental incapacities and be a successful business owner."

—Melissa, 26, New York City

Personality Tests / The Myers–Briggs Type Indicator,
StrengthsFinder, Enneagram, Hogwarts sorting quizzes, BuzzFeed quizzes promising to tell you what kind of off-brand cereal you are—personality tests are *addicting*. From a self-care point of view, you can view quizzes as a fun way to pass time or distract yourself. But you can also view them as a framework for self-knowledge and self-improvement.

Some cynics might say that the urge to take personality quizzes comes from narcissism or the need to define ourselves without doing any of the hard soul-searching. But I respectfully disagree.

Sure, some quizzes aren't overflowing with deep insights about who you are as a person, but a lot of them are surprisingly accurate and can give you a way to understand how you interact with the world, what you need and want out of life, and even how to navigate your weaknesses. In her book *Reading People: How Seeing the World Through the Lens of Personality Changes Everything*, Anne Bogel writes, "I've come to think understanding personality is like a map. That map can't take you anywhere. It doesn't change your location; you're still right where you were before. But the map's purpose isn't to move you; it's to show you the lay of the land. It's the tool that makes it possible for you to get where you want to go."

Pets / We do not deserve pets. The fact that pets grace us with their presence and affection is an inexplicable supernatural phenomenon I will never understand. The self-care benefits of pets go without saying, but I'll say them anyway: They keep you company, are incredible to cuddle with, become your friends, and are *just so cute*.

On a more serious note, though, pets can give you a reason to get up in the morning. You take care of them even when you can't take care of yourself because they're dependent on you. Also, they're a little psychic. If you've ever had an animal place its little paw on you and sit patiently by while you were crying on the floor, you know what I'm talking about.

Of course, I'm not advocating running out and adopting a dog right this second because you're depressed. Owning a pet is a big responsibility that you should think through. When you have a pet,

you have to commit your time, your money, your attention, and maybe sacrifice some of your nice furniture.

All that said, it's not a bad thing if your primary reason for getting a pet is for the mental health benefits. I got my cats because I was feeling incredibly lonely and at a low point in my life, and they've saved me. I love them so much that I've already struck a deal with a demon to ensure their immortality in exchange for my soul.

Plan / Sometimes, you need to go with the flow and take life as

it comes. In general, though, you can make things a lot easier on yourself if you take the time to plan ahead. That doesn't have to mean looking far ahead to the future: Planning your week or even your day in advance keeps you from making decisions based on your mood and falling into a cycle of "I'll do it tomorrow." For tougher activities and errands, like picking up your prescription or getting some exercise, waiting for the mood to strike pretty much guarantees you'll put it off for a long time.

Looking at the big picture is important, too. As Greg McKeown notes in his book *Essentialism*, "When we don't purposely and deliberately choose where to focus our energies and time, other people—our bosses, our colleagues, our clients, and even our families—will choose for us, and before long we'll have lost sight of everything that is meaningful and important." So take the time to plan short-term pleasures and long-term goals so you can make your life what you want it to be.

Their Care: "I'm a really big extrovert, and if I'm alone too often it makes my anxiety and depression so much worse. So I plan little things like movie nights with friends once every week or so, just to make sure I get the social time I need. When life is particularly stressful, I like to have something to look forward to. One of my favorite activities is going to concerts, so I almost always have a concert ticket purchased for a month or two out. That way I always have something fun on the horizon to focus on. Sometimes these are tiny shows of bands I've barely even heard of, but it's a fun way for me to have something exciting to look forward to when everything seems to suck."

—Audrey, 25, Los Angeles, CA

Play / When was the last time you laughed so hard that your lungs rattled against your ribcage? That you had so much fun you lost track of time? That you weren't afraid of looking stupid? Maybe it's been a while. Maybe it feels out of the question, with everything going on. Maybe you just think you're too old.

The thing is, you can be childlike without being childish, so make time to play anyway. It might look different now than it did when you were a child, but the intention can be the same. See if you can't transport yourself back to that feeling of free-spiritedness. Play for the sake of it, with no purpose or ulterior motive other than to open yourself up to joy and to shake the dust off the shelves in your heart to make more room for the beautiful, wonderful, marvelous things your life has to offer. When we're surrounded by darkness, playfulness is an act of resistance. Wield positivity like a weapon and have fun doing it. If you have to play with your kids (or a friend's kid! or a niece or nephew!) to reawaken some childlike wonder in yourself, do it. The parents would probably appreciate a babysitter.

Plants / People spend something like 90 percent of their time indoors.

Knowing what we do about how great nature is for our health, it makes sense that trying to bring some of the outdoors in would give us a boost, too. And according to science, keeping houseplants is actually beneficial for our health in a lot of ways! For one, studies show that plants can actually boost your mood by suppressing the sympathetic nervous system and lowering blood pressure, which lowers stress.

WHICH PLANT IS RIGHT FOR YOU?

❋ If you need a plant that's easy to take care of so you don't kill it and bum yourself out *more*, get an **ALOE PLANT**, a **SPIDER PLANT**, or a **CACTUS**.

❋ If you need to chill out, get a **GARDENIA**. Researchers have found that it might aid in reducing anxiety and have compared its calming fragrance to Valium, which is pretty legit for a plant.

❋ If you want to reap the air-purifying qualities of plants, get a **RUBBER PLANT, ENGLISH IVY,** or a **SNAKE PLANT.** They keep your air clean by removing toxins like benzene, carbon monoxide, and formaldehyde.

❋ If you need help sleeping, get a **SNAKE PLANT** or a **SUCCULENT.** Rather than producing oxygen during the day through photosynthesis like most plants, these do so at night through crassulacean acid metabolism (CAM). And when oxygen levels are increased at night, the air quality goes up, too, and you might get a better night's sleep by reducing snoring or sleep apnea.

❋ Or, you know, just get whatever you find most aesthetically appealing and figure out the rest later!

Playlists / I am a firm believer in the playlist. A playlist holds so

many self-care possibilities. It can score your cinematic wallowing. It can pull you up from the pits of darkness. A good bop infiltrates your soul. The right playlist can really change or set a mood, and can legitimately make the time spent in your home (or your car, or at work) feel more pleasant or meaningful overall.

More than that, though, the act of discovering and listening to new music is an underrated activity to regularly set aside time for. Because do you know what's incredibly lovely? Curling up in bed with headphones on and tea in hand, actively seeking out new music and making playlists.

Plogging / *Plogging*—a Swedish fitness trend

that's a portmanteau of "jogging" and "plocka upp," the Swedish word for "picking up"—combines two things that are wildly good for your mental health: exercise and helping out. In this case, helping out the environment by picking up litter *as* you jog—or walk, cycle, hike, or even paddleboard. The hobby comes with its own community as well; plenty of "ploggers" enjoy posting their loot on social media and comparing trash hauls. And all you need, really, is a trash receptacle and a favorite form of movement.

Power Pose / Picture the character Wonder Woman. Chances are the image that comes to your mind is the Amazonian badass standing with her hands on her hips looking incredibly, well, powerful. It makes sense that channeling similar "powerful" postures might make you feel more confident—and researchers Dana Carney, Amy Cuddy, and Andy Yap hypothesized just that back in a 2010 paper. Striking a ~power pose~ can induce positive hormonal and behavioral changes, and even if you think it's pseudoscience, the placebo effect alone might make it worth trying before a big event or presentation.

Prioritize / Are you focusing your energy on the right things? It's easy to get overwhelmed with the vastness of tasks to accomplish, relationships to maintain, and expectations to meet, but here's the thing—you will never be able to do it all. And that's not meant to be discouraging; it should be freeing. It's a reminder that not everything fighting for your time, energy, and attention deserves it. Some things can wait. Some things don't matter. Some things you can settle for being average at so you have the bandwidth to be incredible at the things that are important to you.

If you were being your happiest self—not the one you beat yourself up for not being, not some idealized version of yourself who does everything perfectly—how would you spend your week? Write it down, down to the hour. When do you work on your passion projects? How often do your see your friends? How many hours of sleep do you get? How do you use your down time? Do you still go to the gym, or do you take that art class instead? How different is this schedule from how you actually spend your time?

Pro-and-Con List / You won't be surprised to hear that, as someone who hasn't *not* been occasionally described as Type A, I'm a big fan of writing lists of pros and cons when it comes to making a decision. I've always employed the good ol' pro-and-con list to help me make rational decisions, both for myself and in helping others: whether to take a job, which project to focus on, whether to dump that person, and so on.

But in dialectical behavioral therapy (DBT), using a pro-and-con list can be applied to the more nebulous, emotional problems and decisions in your life—particularly self-destructive behaviors. When you have an impulsive urge, slow down to make a list about whether you should act on it or tolerate it. For example, I've found it helpful when battling urges to self-harm. Even though the pro ("will be satisfying in the moment") has a strong draw, seeing how the cons outweigh the pro on paper is usually enough to pull me out of it. *See also* Resist Self-Harm.

Puzzles / Doing jigsaw puzzles is a little bit of an old-school hobby, the kind of thing you did at your grandparents' house as a kid. Putting together a puzzle isn't exactly exciting, but you might try giving it a chance if it's been a while or you've never done it. Think about it: It's incredibly satisfying and meditative to turn a disorganized pile of fractions into something lovely and whole when everything else feels like it's falling apart. As writer and friend of mine Rachel W. Miller put it in an essay for BuzzFeed, "A puzzle won't solve all of your problems, but a puzzle is a problem you can solve."

Question / As we've talked about, a major part of CBT is recognizing
that your thoughts are not always true. It may sound simple, but getting
in the habit of fact-checking your thoughts as they occur to you will hone
your ability to quickly shut down negative thoughts.

So, what does that look like?

Opinion: *I'm the worst.*

Fact: *I made a mistake at work that made things harder for my
coworkers.*

Opinion: *I'm going to die alone.*

Fact: *Modern dating is a game of luck and patience, and my singleness is
not a reflection of my worth.*

When you concentrate on facts rather than opinions, you're less likely to beat yourself up—and more likely to give yourself room to problem-solve. Yes, I made a mistake at work, but now I've learned from it and I won't do it again. *See also* Cognitive Distortions.

Their Care: "Self-care is a multifaceted tool I use every day to keep myself alive. My depression/anxiety/PTSD keep what I call Depression Radio going on pretty much 24-7, and play a mix of hits like, 'Everything Is Horrible and No One Likes You,' 'Suicidal Ideation,' 'Every Time I've Misspoken Ever,' and 'Every Awkward Conversation I've Ever Had.' All running on a loop. Combating that is exhausting. Self-care is how I keep it somewhat in check. There are dozens of large and small things I do as self-care and I could go on for hours on how I work them into life, but what it means to me in the largest sense is the fundamental idea that I am worthy of care and kindness."

—Crista Anne, 36, Chesapeake, VA

Quiet / Having background noise—in the form of crowds, music, Netflix reruns, whatever—is the default. Carve out quiet time for existing without distraction. See what thoughts occur to you in the silence, or what sounds you notice that you'd normally filter out.

Quote / Quotes can seem sort of cheesy . . . until you find the exact perfect quote that speaks to your heart and/or lights a fire under your ass. So start a quote collection on your phone or in your journal and give it a read when you need a little affirmation.

WAKE UP EVERY
MORNING AND TELL
YOURSELF THAT
YOU'RE A BADASS
BITCH FROM HELL
AND THAT NO ONE
CAN FUCK WITH YOU
AND THEN DON'T LET
ANYBODY FUCK
WITH YOU.

—KATE NASH

Radical Acceptance / When you run into a problem, you

usually cycle through a few options. First, you try to figure out if it's
a solvable problem. If it is, great. If it's not, you try to change your
perception of it. But sometimes that doesn't work, either. At that
point, you *basically* have two choices: You can continue to ruminate on
it, or you can decide to practice what is known as "radical acceptance."

Typically used in DBT, radical acceptance is the practice of
acknowledging that sometimes the only thing you can do in the face
of a problem is accept the reality of your situation. Which, I know, is
easier said than done. By giving yourself permission to accept things
as they are, you give yourself space to start to move on.

To be clear, accepting doesn't mean agreeing with or condoning or ignoring your emotions about a situation. Accepting that your friend is not going to make an effort to regain your trust after betraying you is not agreeing with what she did. Accepting that you are stuck in bumper-to-bumper traffic and will be late to work is not deciding that the situation isn't frustrating and annoying—it's just shifting your thinking away from frustration and annoyance because it won't help.

Make sure to give yourself time to make it to the acceptance stage—it doesn't come automatically. Just as you have to go through denial, anger, bargaining, and depression when grieving before you can reach acceptance, you have to explore solutions and even give yourself time to be optimistic that things will change on their own. Otherwise, it will ring false.

> # By giving yourself permission to accept things as they are, you give yourself space to start to move on.

Reach Out to Someone You Love / It doesn't
have to be a big deal, and it can be through a text or a phone call or whatever. Just talk to someone you like, about anything. Remember it's always an option.

Their Care: "As someone with fibromyalgia and arthritis, self-care is not holding myself to able-bodied standards. It is giving my body rests and breaks when I need them, not when I absolutely shut down. I'm someone who tends to tie a lot of my self-worth to my productivity, which gets difficult when you can barely endure sitting because of pain, let alone using your hands to create. I'm always struggling against the idea that I should just keep going. I get angry at myself and my body for being in pain, and it's easy to fall into a trap of pushing myself forward. Self-care is the simple act of listening to my body and responding appropriately, even if it's not the norm. It's reminding myself that days off and times of rest are not a luxury, they are an absolute necessity."

—**Peter, 24, Boston, MA**

Read / There are few activities that promise a distraction as immersive, rewarding, and entertaining as reading. Read books, articles, comic books, blog posts, and poems. Read far and wide and expand your world one page at a time. Read the stuff you *actually* like and don't force yourself to finish a book you aren't feeling. Life's too short!

Recalibrate / Your mental health is going to evolve and change throughout your life—and your self-care routine will have to evolve, too. If something that once worked extremely well for calming you down doesn't seem as effective anymore, it might be time to go back to the experimental phase. Keep in mind that you might still *enjoy* that activity, even if it's not as effective anymore. No one says you need to stop! You might just want to pick another go-to ~calming~ activity when it comes to self-care.

Recovery Time / I can't count how many times, in a fit of
optimism, I've booked my weekends with back-to-back plans. *Of course I can go straight from brunch with Matt and Alanna to a movie with Anne. And after that, I can totally meet up with Caitlin for dinner.* Every! Time! And as you can imagine, that never works out and I wind up canceling half of my plans the day of and feeling like a gigantic flake.

We all get drained after stimulating events because it's impossible to stay in an ongoing state of emotional and physiological arousal without burning out. Carve out time to catch your breath, whether it's chilling in your car for an extra fifteen minutes before leaving work to go home to your kids or a midday nap between your brunch and night plans. If you're always *go-go-go*, you'll wind up sucking the joy out of even those activities you enjoy.

Their Care: "I am a partner in a home daycare business and I work fifty to sixty hours a week. I'm with kids and people all day long and the noise alone gets overwhelming at times. Taking time for myself to breathe and relax and not worry about work or the dishes in the sink, or whatever, has saved me from a breakdown more times than I can count. Before I started taking self-care seriously, I was so easily annoyed and always frustrated in every aspect of my life, constantly feeling like I just wanted to scream. Sometimes self-care is turning the music up loud in my car and screaming. It's about balance."

—Katie, 27, Merced, CA

Reframe / A tiny but significant way to naturally recalibrate your mind toward positivity is to tweak the language you use to express yourself. There are certain phrases that carry negative weight, even if you don't realize it, and when you shift your phrasing away from tiny negativities, you wind up feeling more gratitude, optimism, and happiness. Here's what that looks like:

- **REPLACE "I'M SORRY" WITH "THANK YOU."** Instead of saying, "Sorry I'm late," say, "Thanks for waiting for me." Or instead of saying, "Sorry I'm in a bad mood today," say, "Thank you for being patient with me." Obviously, there will always be things that call for an apology, but if you find yourself saying sorry a lot, this might help shift your thinking to be more positive and make sure your loved ones get your gratitude instead of your negativity.

- **REPLACE "BUT" WITH "AND."** Often when we use "but" we're implying, even unconsciously, that two things are mutually exclusive. Or we put undue focus on the "but." For instance, if you're stressing out about an upcoming interview, you might rant to friends and say something like "I'm so excited for the chance, but I am so nervous I'll mess up." It may seem small, but when you swap it with "I'm so excited for the chance and I'm so nervous I'll mess up," you make room for both emotions, both points of view, both truths. Nerves don't trump excitement.

- **REPLACE "I HAVE TO" WITH "I GET TO."** It can help you think of your crowded schedule in a more positive light. Busyness stress can make you forget that your schedule is actually packed with things you genuinely enjoy, such as hanging out with friends, going to the gym, and fitting in time for your hobbies. If you anticipate something being stressful, it probably will be, but if you look at commitments as opportunities and remind yourself that, yes, some of them are fun, they immediately become less physically and mentally taxing.

Relieve / Check in with yourself and find out what aches and pains you haven't been tending to. A good way to do this is through a body scan meditation. Before the word "meditation" scares you off, this is basically an excuse to lie on the floor and do nothing—but in a way that weirdly works wonders when you're stressed. The exercise is meant to get you in touch with your body by mindfully relaxing it from head to toe. What does that mean, exactly? It mostly means paying attention: to sensations, to tension, to pressure.

Start by lying down on your back or whatever posture is comfortable for you. Beginning with the top of your head or the tips of your toes, focus your awareness on one part of your body at a time. As you move from one body part to another, pay attention to the sensations you feel: muscle tightness, temperature, buzzing, aching, tingling, pressure, or nothing at all.

This might just be a good grounding meditation when you're otherwise feeling anxious, but it could also lead to awareness and discovery. Are you holding tension in your shoulders? Do you clench your jaw? Has pain snuck into your knees when you weren't paying attention? What can you do to relieve these pains?

CHECK IN WITH
YOURSELF AND
FIND OUT WHAT
ACHES AND PAINS
YOU HAVEN'T BEEN
TENDING TO.

Their Care: "I've been having a hard time figuring out my own gender, and as I've been working through my gender identity, I've fought my natural instinct to keep every part of my evolving feelings sealed away, especially from my partner. One of the most helpful things I learned through therapy (which I was really reluctant to start at first) was how to talk to other people, through the sometimes-physical manifestations of my anxieties. Like saying, 'My limbs are starting to tingle, I think I'm about to have a panic attack. Could you breathe with me or give me a hand to hold?' or 'I'm tearing up in reaction to something going on in my head.' The hardest thing for me to overcome was learning how to express my need for a certain kind of care without instinctively blaming myself or the people around me for the fact of that need."

—Lio, 26, Alameda, CA

Reminisce / How often do you let yourself flip through the past?

We're told all the time not to dwell there and sometimes we forget to live in the present, but that doesn't mean we can't visit. In fact, we owe it to ourselves to occasionally dig up long-buried memories, dust them off, and hold them up to the light so they can shine on us again. It would be a waste not to recycle past happiness when it's right there for the taking.

Be careful, though: Sometimes it's easy to fall into the trap of feeling sad when reminiscing about happy memories. Relationships that are no longer in your life, ages that you'll never return to, history that is bittersweet to revisit. As you hold space for relics of the past that once brought you joy and fulfillment, remind yourself that endings aren't failures. At any given moment, you might be living through something you'll one day miss, so give your future self permission to look back on today with fondness and do the same for your present self in the meantime.

The past dwells in all sorts of nooks and crannies: journals, social media accounts, camera rolls on your phone, mementos shoved into the back of your junk drawer. You'd be shocked what jogs your memory. Ask your friends and loved ones to reminisce with you—their favorite stories could very well be portals to worlds you've already forgotten.

Resist Self-Harm / Self-harm or self-injury refers to hurting

yourself on purpose and is associated with various mental illnesses, trauma, or abuse. The urge to self-harm isn't uncommon, but just because it isn't uncommon doesn't mean it's a healthy coping mechanism or that recovery isn't possible. Recovery is different for everyone and can be a long process involving the help of a professional, but in the meantime, find what helps you resist the urge to self-harm. A lot of the self-care tools outlined in this book are great distractions and alternatives, such as knitting and other hobbies that keep your hands busy and your emotions bearable. But there are also some more tactile coping methods that people who self-harm find helpful, too—such as drawing on the skin you'd normally injure or splashing cold water on your face. The more alternatives you have, the better.

Reward / Sometimes you have to bribe yourself to do things that are

good for you. It's OK. Some things that are good for you *aren't very fun*, so you have to create the incentive for yourself. (People who do everything they're supposed to just because they know it's good for them are the types who survive the apocalypse. Or witches.) Rewards can be anything from treating yourself to ~the fancy candle~ to giving yourself a weekend off to marathon that show you've been meaning to watch.

Sometimes you have to bribe yourself to do things that are good for you.

Their Care: "I've designated this year the Year of Self-Care and in order to achieve that, I am giving myself star stickers (yes, stickers!) on my calendar for every self-care activity that I do. Or, at least, every time I do one of the five I've designated as something I want to focus on for this year. I still do other forms of self-care, too, but it was important for me to focus on these five."

—Irina, 33, Fort Myers, FL

Rom-Coms / Romantic comedies transport you to a world where everything is bright and shiny, and the worst conflicts are minor misunderstandings that can be smoothed over with a grand gesture. It's the visual equivalent of grocery store fondant sugar cookies. It's balm for the soul.

Routines / There's comfort and joy in routines, particularly

ones that we've designed ourselves, with our specific needs in mind. And, of course, figuring out what your self-care routine looks like is kind of the whole point here. So don't feel like you have to constantly be trying something new and exciting; sticking with what works is perfectly fine. Two of the best types of routines to have—in my humble opinion, anyway—are a solid morning routine and a relaxing nighttime routine, to help you wake up and wind down.

Their Care: "My self-care routine has changed over the years, but here's the current iteration for every night: Turn on lava lamp, take a shower, do skin care routine, put on smelly lotion, turn on my electric blanket, lie in my bed, cross-stitch and watch an episode of TV, and watch the lava lamp. Then I turn everything off and go to bed. I had no idea how much I would love the lava lamp when I got it, and now I turn it on every night."

—Suzanne, 25, Memphis, TN

Safety Outfit / When I wake up on a bad mental health day, getting out of bed is like scaling a mountain—so much so that once I do it, I don't have much energy left to put into getting ready for the day. This is fine in theory, because I don't necessarily *want* to care about what I look like, but I always wind up feeling worse when I later realize how uncomfortable I am being out and about looking as bad as I feel. So I try to have a few reliable outfits that are (1) comfortable and (2) make me feel good about myself—I know I can grab those on bad days without any effort. What ~safety~ feels like for you will undoubtedly be different, but whatever it is, it's a worthy investment.

Scent Therapy / When it comes to the so-called benefits of aromatherapy and essential oils, the science isn't *really* there, but for some people, certain scents *do* inspire certain moods and mind-sets. You can incorporate scents into your self-care routine in the form of lotions, essential oils, candles, or diffusers if it works for you.

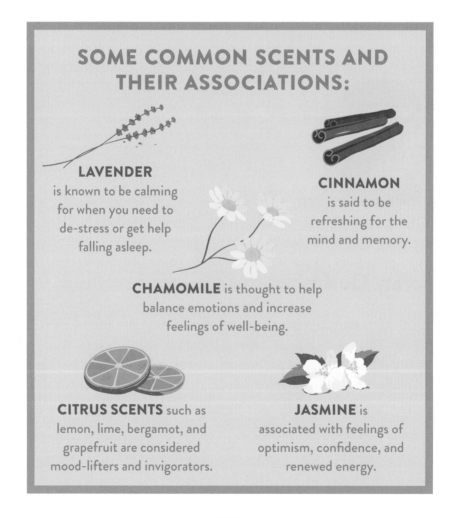

SOME COMMON SCENTS AND THEIR ASSOCIATIONS:

LAVENDER is known to be calming for when you need to de-stress or get help falling asleep.

CINNAMON is said to be refreshing for the mind and memory.

CHAMOMILE is thought to help balance emotions and increase feelings of well-being.

CITRUS SCENTS such as lemon, lime, bergamot, and grapefruit are considered mood-lifters and invigorators.

JASMINE is associated with feelings of optimism, confidence, and renewed energy.

Self-Compassion / For a lot of us, having compassion for others comes naturally, but when it comes to applying the same kindness to ourselves, our minds short-circuit and it feels *impossible*. Luckily, self-compassion is a skill you can cultivate through practice. You can start by simply acknowledging when you're having a hard time. When you're struggling, take a moment to recognize your feelings. Like, "Wow, this is a really shitty situation and I am right to feel hurt." Or if you did something that you're beating yourself up for, remind yourself that you're only human: "I shouldn't have snapped at my girlfriend, but my chronic pain was really bad and my patience was thin. I can apologize."

> # When you're struggling, take a moment to recognize your feelings.

Their Care: "Honestly, self-care is as fraught a concept as any I've encountered in mental health. Is sleeping for twelve hours self-care or depression? If I light a candle for self-care, is that OK or have I propped up capitalism? If I stay in on a Friday night and watch Netflix is that self-care or am I avoiding the socializing I need to make a connection that will stave off the worst of my depression? Am I giving into my anxiety? I suppose I practice self-care by doing my best to say, 'Fuck it, I'm going to do this thing and try not to overthink it.'"

—Sarah, 40, Windsor, NY

Self-Esteem / Speaking of self-compassion, according to Dr.
Guy Winch, increasing self-compassion also helps increase self-esteem, which is *massively* important for all sorts of mental health reasons. In *Emotional First Aid*, he writes, "[Low self-esteem] renders us more vulnerable to many of the psychological injuries we sustain in daily life, such as failure or rejection. [People with low self-esteem] also have worse moods; they face a greater risk of depression, anxiety, and eating disorders; and they experience their relationships as less fulfilling than people with higher self-esteem do."

So how do you actually increase self-esteem? It's not exactly easy, but research has found it *is* possible. One of the most straightforward things you can do, according to Dr. Winch, is to write down a list of your best attributes and qualities, and choose one to write a brief essay of appreciation about. Going forward, you can continue writing about each of the qualities you came up with until you make your way through the list and find yourself a lot more receptive to appreciating yourself.

Self-Talk / Sometimes when you're having irrational, unhelpful, or negative thoughts, you have to literally talk yourself out of it. *Firmly.* I've been collecting my favorite self-talk statements from worksheets I've gotten in therapy over the years, and I keep them in my Bullet Journal for reference. Here are some that I find particularly helpful when my brain is acting up that you might want to steal:

- *"I've done the best I can."*

- *"I can cope with this."*

- *"I don't have to figure out this problem right this minute. The best thing to do is just drop it for now."*

- *"That thought isn't helpful right now."*

- *"Now is not the time to think about it. I can think about it later."*

- *"I'm ready to move on now."*

- *"I can handle being wrong."*

- *"This is irrational. I'm going to let it go."*

- *"I won't argue with an irrational thought."*

- *"I already know from my past experiences that these fears are irrational."*

- *"This is not an emergency. I can slow down and think clearly about what I need."*

- *"This feels threatening and urgent, but it really isn't."*

- *"I don't have to be perfect to be OK."*

- *"It's OK to make mistakes."*

Shift / How open are you to change? Do you back yourself into corners by being too rigid to switch directions? What boxes could you get out of if you only thought to angle yourself a little differently? Moving through the world requires constant recalibration. Just as you think you've figured it out, the world will hurl something unexpected at you—and if you are too stuck in your own way of doing things, you will take the blows. Being resolute in our beliefs is a good thing, but if we're not also flexible when necessary, that resolve will harden into a stubbornness that will keep us from growing—and even leave us in harm's way.

When you run into roadblocks or things that make you want to crumble, remember that point of view can be everything. Shifting perspectives, shifting tactics, shifting paths—none of it has to mean becoming someone you're not or looking blindly on the bright side. After all, silver linings can be impossible to see in the dark. When you give yourself permission to be flexible, you learn to nimbly navigate curveballs, handle disappointment with grace, and forge your own path toward the light.

Show Up / From time to time, the thought of being social is so preemptively exhausting that we forget we have the option of just showing up and being a little boring. You don't have to plan on being a social butterfly; tag along with a group of friends you love and who love you, and just exist with them. Listen in on conversations. Bask in the energy. That counts, too.

Sick Days / It is depressing that I consistently have to remind myself that my sick days are for me to use, but burnout culture is a powerful drug. If you have the privilege of paid sick days, don't be a hero by going in to work and powering through an illness. And even if you don't have sick days, if you're sick and can swing it financially (and I know the reality is that not everyone can), you should prioritize getting better. Pushing yourself to work before you're recovered usually means you'll wind up sick for *longer*.

Skin Care / Anyone who is really into skin care will tell you that it's about more than hygiene: It's a lifestyle and a coping mechanism. As the world explodes around us, taking care of your skin is a small, controllable project you can take on. Writer Jia Tolentino aptly summarizes the draw of taking obsessive care of our skin in *The New Yorker*, calling it a "psychological safety blanket."

And it's a pretty simple security blanket, all things considered: It's a small ritual of self-love that gives your brain a mindfulness break while also yielding physical benefits. When your skin feels and looks healthy, you wind up feeling better too. Not to mention that your skin is your largest organ and it keeps all your blood and guts and muscles from spilling out. You owe it to that miraculous meat sack to take good care of it.

Smile / Research shows that a genuine smile can actually make you less stressed. So smile at your barista, accept compliments, watch a Disney movie—whatever gets you grinning. Or, you know, you could even try fake smiling until a real one kicks in.

Splurge / There are times when spending a little bit more money is a worthy price for saving yourself time, peace of mind, or unhappiness. Obviously, it's a huge privilege to be able to splurge, but if you have it in your budget to throw money at a problem that would genuinely make your life a little easier, it might be the solution you've been looking for.

For me, that means sometimes getting my groceries delivered. I know that eating junk exacerbates my depression tenfold, yet I'm quick to order delivery when I don't have the time or energy to go grocery shopping. But sometimes I let myself order my groceries online because it guarantees I'll eat healthfully when I'm in a funk, which helps me get out of it faster.

For you, that could mean splurging on laundry pickup and delivery so you have fresh clothes. Or it could mean paying someone to clean your place when it turns into a depression cave and the thought of having to do it yourself is overwhelming. Or joining a group training class at your gym because you need help motivating yourself. Or taking a cab to your friend's house because you want to be around people but taking the bus would be too draining. Sometimes taking care of yourself involves weighing monetary costs against the cost of time or energy.

SOMETIMES
TAKING CARE OF
YOURSELF INVOLVES
WEIGHING MONETARY
COSTS AGAINST
THE COST OF TIME
OR ENERGY.

Their Care: "Self-care, to me, means anything that makes me feel like me. It isn't something I thought about until recently, when I was diagnosed with PCOS (polycystic ovary syndrome). Side effects that I have include missed periods, fluctuating weight loss/gain (but mostly gain), and very high testosterone levels. For a long time, doctors told me my symptoms weren't a big deal, that I could live with it, making me feel like I deserved all this. Before being diagnosed, I just thought I was cursed with the facial (and other) hair of a man. I would have to shave my face twice a day—sometimes more. And I never really felt like a woman until I started laser hair removal last year, because for the first time I could afford it. It is expensive, painful, and smells weird, but it's worked and for the first time in my life I feel like a woman. This is my self-care!"

—Carrie, 29, Brooklyn, NY

Spruce Up / Do whatever you need to be really feelin' yourself.

Put on your favorite outfit. Do a deep-dive into makeup and hair tutorials on YouTube and give them your best shot. Play with your gender expression. Try your hand at stage or costume makeup to see if you can completely transform yourself. Take a million selfies so your camera roll becomes a beautiful mosaic of your beautiful face. It doesn't even have to be about *you*. The care and precision that go into beautifying—or uglifying or transforming or *whatever*—is an art and a skill to be cultivated.

Their Care: "I'm trans, and I have a history of body dysmorphia (intrusive thoughts where I imagine or blow up faults in my appearance) and dysphoria (anxiety and stress surrounding gender, specifically around the discomfort with one's assigned gender at birth). For me, I get most dysphoric about my face and chest when I am unable to bind. When my dysphoria and dysmorphia act up, it's very difficult to recognize myself in the mirror. My face and my body seem to change every few minutes, in every reflection. It's not uncommon for me to think I'm de-transitioning, or that my weight has suddenly changed.

Between my dysmorphia and dysphoria, a lot of self-care is tied to making myself look nice (for me!). My dysphoria and dysmorphia are unfortunately woven together, so when I'm struggling it helps to do my full face. When I first started transitioning, makeup was essential for getting through the day—it was how I could actually look masculine by contouring and playing down my "feminine" features. Now, one or two years on testosterone, doing my regular makeup is always a pick-me-up when my dysphoria acts up."

—**Mars, 19, Portland, OR**

Stargaze / We have *no* idea how many stars are in the known universe, just that they're uncountable and every star we can see in the night sky is bigger and brighter than our sun. The closest star to us, after the sun, is about *25 trillion miles* away. That's 25,000,000,000,000 miles. With the sky at our disposal, this monstrous and beautiful tapestry that is completely unfathomable, we have a way to tap into awe and wonder whenever we need to get outside ourselves. Look up. Hunt for constellations. Ponder the universe. Or just think, *Holy shit, I'm tiny.* Not only will it be an opportunity to relax and spend time in nature, but it might just make your problems feel a bit smaller—and a bit more manageable.

Start Over / A lot of things can get in the way of getting off a path, even once you realize it's the wrong one: pride, investment, obligation, fear. But the longer you put off starting over, or trying something new, or making a big change, the more difficult it will be—and it *will* catch up with you. This could mean changing jobs or locations, breaking up with a long-term partner, making all new friends, *whatever*. You wouldn't be alone: According to the US Bureau of Labor Statistics, the average American changes jobs ten to fifteen times between the ages of eighteen and forty-six. It's not easy. It's *so* not easy. But if your gut is telling you that you're not living the life you want, you have to give yourself permission to make a change.

Their Care: "I had just graduated from college, and returned to my hometown in Florida after my post-grad adventure across the country at Mount Rainier. Feeling suffocated by family expectations and unable to truly be myself in my hometown, I chose to make the move to Seattle, WA, with my boyfriend. That was the biggest act of self-care I could have possibly done for myself. While I love my family and do wish I could see them more frequently, living in Seattle has helped me so much. A lot of my friends and family were completely baffled—and some were hurt—by my choice to move to Seattle. Self-care, to me, means that sometimes people may view your choices as selfish."

—Kristen, 24, Seattle, WA

Stop Judging What Works for You / It's freeing to admit that you'll never be the type of person whose regular self-care routine involves yoga, meditation, and a nightly cup of calming tea. If you *are* that person, then more power to you. But the image of the picture-perfect healthy self-care routine that the media perpetuates doesn't work for everyone. So don't hold yourself to a standard of what you think self-care *should* look like. Find what works for you and enjoy it without shame or judgment.

Support Group / Friends are great, but it can also be incredibly

healing to seek out a group of people who are going through the same things you are. There are a lot of support groups out there—groups for people with specific mental illnesses and chronic conditions, groups for grief, recovery groups, queer groups, anger management groups, groups for family and friends of those who are suffering, the list goes on. *Psychology Today*'s group therapy and support group finder is a good place to start.

Their Care: "I practice self-care in a weird way. I lock myself in a bathroom with my food and laptop, then I do random stuff in the mirror like give myself a pep talk, dance horribly, etc. I think self-care means giving yourself more positivity."

—Ash, 14, United States

Swap Tips / When you connect with people who have gone

through what you're struggling with, you can feel so much less alone—and get some advice based on personal experience and trial and error. Ask people who are dealing with similar issues what they do, whether that means asking people who have the same illness you do, people who share your sexuality or gender identity, fellow activists, or people in your profession. People who have been there have the best advice.

Talk About Your Feelings / As hard as it can be to open up, talking about what you're feeling can really lighten your load. The more you express your true feelings with other people, the more they share back, and the more you realize that we all kind of have the same insecurities and hang-ups and fears. Everyone ruminates on the tiniest shit, even when it's irrational. Everyone gets hit with impostor syndrome and feels like they have no idea what they're doing. Everyone, at some point or another, fears that other people wouldn't like them if they knew who they *really* were behind their public mask.

When you learn these things, you're less likely to take things personally and internalize the comments and behaviors of other people. So many of us are acting out of our own vulnerabilities and you only see that once you start finding common ground.

Tarot / The tarot is a deck of seventy-eight cards, each with its own story, symbolism, and meaning. Everyone reads tarot differently, with their own methods and spreads, but for most people, you pose a question or situation, draw cards, and put them in a formation (or a spread) where each position represents a different aspect of the answer. Tarot has a reputation for being all about ~fortune-telling~ and predicting the future, and while some people use tarot that way, that's only the tip of the iceberg. Many more use tarot as a tool to make choices, manifest goals, and learn about themselves, making it one of my favorite tools for self-care.

Sometimes you feel weird focusing on yourself or putting your problems front and center, and if that's the case, the ritual of reading tarot cards gives you permission to be intentional about it. Practicing tarot is, in many ways, inherently meditative and therapeutic. It's a shortcut for tapping into your intuition and gut. It's a way to reflect on yourself, your life, and your needs, as well as a means by which to get distance from yourself and your problems, untangle unhelpful thoughts and narratives, and clarify your values and priorities. All while feeling a little bit magical.

HOW TO START
READING TAROT

For beginner readers, three-card spreads are straightforward and accessible. All you need is a deck and access to the internet where you can look up the meanings of the cards. Hey, we all have to start somewhere. Here are some common three-card spreads to get you started:

JUSTICE	THE MOON	THE WORLD
Past	Present	Future
Current situation	Obstacle	Advice
The problem	Do this	Don't do this
Who I think I am	Who others think I am	Who I really am
Option 1	Option 2	Option 3

Tea / Hot leaf water shouldn't have the soothing powers that it does, but . . . it *does*. Loose-leaf, bag, herbal, black—brewing a cup never fails to create a small pocket of peace in the chaotic world. And there might actually be a scientific reason for that; a cup of warm anything in your hands mimics human warmth, which is said to have calming properties. So not only does a properly brewed cup of tea transport you—it can be a winter vacation in a mug, a sweater on a crisp, chill day, a cozy night by the fire, a storm from beneath a warm blanket—it is also a pretty good stand-in for human comfort. Just don't forget about it and let it go cold.

Teach / What are you the group chat expert in? What hobbies have you been doing for ages? What are your secret talents? Whatever you have a knack for, there's bound to be someone out there who wants to learn it, too. It could be as simple as showing your coworker the best hacks on Excel. On top of giving you something to do and getting you out of your own head (hello, distraction), you also get the boost of their gratitude and the feeling of your own utility and expertise. We all like to feel useful sometimes.

Therapy / The very act of allowing yourself a space to focus on you and only you is one of the most compassionate things you can do for yourself—but it feels weird. We're all used to relationships being reciprocal, a balance between talking and listening, venting and helping. Which is what makes having a therapist so magical. Yes, it's a professional relationship, but it's also a weird, wonderful, intimate one, probably unlike any other connection you have. Here's this person in your corner whose job it is to be an expert at supporting you. Where else can you get that?

For more information on therapy, see Therapy FAQs, page 220.

TIPP / TIPP stands for Temperature, Intense exercise, Paced breathing, and Paired muscle relaxation, and it's another distress tolerance skill from DBT to put in your toolkit. You can whip it out when you're at an emotional breaking point or just feel *really overwhelmed*. To break it down:

Temperature: When we're upset, our temperatures tend to rise, so holding an ice cube, splashing water on the face, blasting the AC, or taking a cool shower are all solid ways to cool down. And when you cool down physically, you cool down emotionally, too.

Intense exercise: Exhausting your body is a good way to pull focus away from your mind and your emotions. Not only does increasing oxygen flow help reduce stress levels, it also gives you a place to channel your intense emotions.

Paced breathing: Steady breathing helps your body chill out, so focus on your breathing pattern—using whatever technique is most comfortable for you—until you start to calm down.

Paired muscle relaxation: When you tighten your muscles, such as in your arms, and then relax them, the muscles become *even more relaxed* than they were before. In turn, relaxed muscles don't need as much oxygen, so your heart rate and breathing will slow, too. Bodies are wild! Try tightening a group of muscles as much as you can for five seconds, then let them relax. You'll probably feel yourself relaxing, too.

Their Care: "I recently learned that I'm experiencing postpartum depression. Life completely changed when I became a mom. I didn't realize just how much—or that I was no longer practicing self-care—until little changes in my personality became bigger and more noticeable. Little things that didn't used to bother me suddenly bother me a lot. Things that used to bring me joy no longer do. Friends that I used to pursue to catch up and hang out with now have to pursue me because I'm too tapped out to initiate relationships. Self-care allows me to have the capacity for those things. Self-care is a 'Which came first, the chicken or the egg?' situation, and the answer is, 'Yes.'"

—Taiko, 30, Visalia, CA

Touch / There's a term for the feeling of being touch-starved: "skin hunger." While this might sound like it's associated with zombies and cannibals, it's actually a very real phenomenon some psychologists use to describe the need for physical contact. As humans, we long for physical touch—and there's a whole bunch of research out there about its benefits, and what happens when we go without it.

Take, for example, the controversial experiments run by American psychologist Harry Harlow: Infant monkeys were separated from their birth mothers and given the choice between two fake moms. One was made out of wood and wire, and the other was covered in cloth. Overwhelmingly, the baby monkeys went for the soft, comforting fake mom—even when the one made of wood and water held a bottle of milk. From Harlow's research, it's now generally accepted that we need touch almost as much as we need basic necessities like food and water.

Gary Chapman also emphasizes the importance of physical contact in his book *The 5 Love Languages*, in which he argues that people have five main ways they prefer to receive love, one of them being touch. Also, touch releases oxytocin, a hormone that produces pleasure, bonding, and even antidepressive effects.

It might go without saying that comfort contact is a very healing form of self-care. The tough part is that we live in an increasingly disconnected world (loneliness is now considered more of an epidemic than ever before). Not only that, but opportunities for physical contact may be rare unless you have a regular romantic partner or partners, a close relationship with your parents or your own kids, or a particularly touchy-feely group of friends.

There are ways to satisfy skin hunger if you don't have any obvious avenues for it in your day-to-day life. Think: getting a professional massage, playing contact sports, cuddling pets, volunteering with elderly people who need physical assistance. And consider floating the idea of cuddling by your friends. They might be just as touch-deprived as you are.

Track Your Habits and Moods / When you keep track of your habits and how you feel physically and mentally, you can start to play detective and make connections—meaning you can look back and say, *OK, I did this and felt good, and I did that and felt bad*. This can help you practice more effective self-care in the long run.

There are habit-tracking and mood-tracking apps out there, but for me, there's nothing quite like a good ol' tracker in my Bullet Journal where I can physically check off each habit every day and look at big-picture patterns every month. There's really no limit to what you can track: moods, pain, hours of sleep, water intake, alcohol consumption; if you socialized, if you exercised, if you took your meds. The act of tracking will help you remember to *do the thing* in the first place. If you're anything like me, the satisfaction of building up a streak is enough to help maintain a healthy habit. *See also* Bullet Journal.

Their Care: "I'm Sicilian, with a slightly overbearing, well-intentioned, but frustratingly out-of-touch mother who really wanted me married and pregnant *yesterday*. She wants grandbabies. I want to find a way to afford them first. Not to mention a partner who doesn't ghost me on OkCupid after a week of mindless conversation. I take myself on a date once every couple of months that's just me, a bowl of good ramen, and a reasonably priced massage. It's fair to say with the state of my dating life (nonexistent) and my general trust issues (there are many, stemming from a sometimes crippling lack of self-confidence and body issues) that I'm pretty touch-starved. The intimacy of a massage is relaxing and soothing because it fulfills something that I didn't even realize I was missing until I sat down and did a lot of self-reflection."

—Kristina, 29, New York City

Understand Your Anger / Anger is an emotion that

you can soothe with self-care, but it's kind of a tricky one—because sometimes what seems like anger isn't actually anger at all. For a lot of people, anger is a knee-jerk response to cover up more vulnerable emotions like guilt, sadness, fear, or hurt. It's a *classic* defense mechanism. So when it comes time to figure out how you're going to practice self-care in the face of feeling pissed off, it's worth interrogating the emotion a little bit. Are you actually mad? Because if not, you might have to change tactics when it comes to deciding what form of self-care will be most effective.

SOME IDEAS FOR COPING WITH ANGER, IF THAT IS INDEED WHAT YOU'RE DEALING WITH:

- **LEAVE AN ENVIRONMENT.** There's a reason movie and TV characters are always like, "I need some air" when their temper is about to boil over. Because that shit works!

- **CHECK IN TO SEE IF YOU NEED TO EAT.** You're probably familiar with the feeling of hanger—hunger plus anger—but did you know it's an actual physiological response to wanting food? Basically, when your blood sugar drops, your cortisol and adrenaline levels go up, and your brain secretes neuropeptides that control the brain's chemicals. And the ones that trigger hunger and the ones that trigger anger are the same, making the reactions similar, too.

- **COMFORT YOUR INNER CHILD.** Thich Nhat Hanh, a Vietnamese Buddhist monk and peace activist, dispenses this advice in his book *Anger: Wisdom for Cooling the Flames*: "Anger is like a howling baby, suffering and crying. The baby needs his mother to embrace him. You are the mother for your baby, your anger. The moment you begin to practice breathing mindfully in and out, you have the energy of a mother, to cradle and embrace the baby. Just embracing your anger, just breathing in and breathing out, that is good enough. The baby will feel relief right away."

- **WRITE THAT ANGRY LETTER—BUT DON'T SEND IT.** Sometimes you need to get your nasty out in a way that doesn't hurt other people, so don't hold back—let out your feelings, your petty and childish thoughts, empty them out of your head and onto the page to see if it helps.

Unfollow / Why do we hate-follow people on social media?

Sometimes it can be entertaining to see what wild thing a politician tweeted now, or maybe you feel compulsively compelled to stay up to date on your ex just to make sure you're still winning. You probably know in your heart of hearts that there's no real upside to hate-following besides the instant gratification of quenching your curiosity. And if you were being completely honest with yourself, you'd probably agree it's doing your mental health more harm than good.

The people you hate-follow aren't the only ones you should get off your feed for your mental health, though. There might also be people who just make you feel . . . bad, insecure, jealous, annoyed, left out, whatever. For example, it's OK to unfollow a friend whom you're starting to like a little less because of their social media persona, and you want to preserve your friendship. Do it! You're not obligated to follow *anyone*.

Besides the obvious unfollowing and unplugging completely, there are steps you can take to make your social media spaces more positive— and to improve your relationship with technology in general:

- **TECH-FREE MORNINGS.** I'm not someone who finds it easy to cut down on my tech use. For better or for worse, I'm attached to my phone and my laptop. So for the reluctant unpluggers like me, I recommend taking the baby step of not checking your phone first thing in the morning. Reaching for it is more automatic than satisfying, so it didn't take very long for me to break the habit once I started paying attention.

- **MUTING.** For a million unspoken social etiquette rules, both ridiculous and legit, unfollowing someone is more complicated than just clicking a button. Following someone on platforms like Twitter and Instagram has become a significant part of friendship. So unfollowing someone—just like bumping someone off your Myspace Top 8 back in the days of yore—can seem like a statement. The easiest solution to sidestep drama or misunderstandings is muting. You get to cleanse your feed, and no one but you has to know.

- **DISABLE PUSH NOTIFICATIONS.** Or at least cut down on them and curate them significantly. So many of us are accustomed to reaching for our phone whenever it buzzes with a text, email, news alert, or follower alert. We do it without thinking! Cutting down on notifications makes you more mindful and deliberate about when you check your phone. You'll be surprised how often you'll forget to check it for long stretches of time without it screaming for your attention with notifications.

- **SOFT BLOCKING.** Look, sometimes someone winds up following you on Twitter or Instagram whom you don't want keeping tabs on your posts. Maybe it's a well-intentioned but nosy extended-family member who isn't satisfied with just being friends on Facebook, or maybe it's a particularly annoying commenter or reply guy. Soft blocking—blocking and then immediately unblocking someone so they're forced to unfollow you—is less drastic and detectable than a permanent block. They might not even notice.

Unplug / People put their happiest selves forward on social media—
relationships, vacations, work brags, etc.—which makes it easy to wind up feeling like shit about your own life. Step away and focus more on the IRL, especially when you're feeling your mental health drag. Also be aware of how being plugged in creates a ton of inputs (all those different tabs, apps, multiple screens at once!) that can leave you feeling scattered, stressed, anxious, overwhelmed, and unable to enjoy much of anything. So experiment with unplugging regularly—fifteen minutes before bed, during your commute, for an hour a day—and see how it makes you feel.

Their Care: "Twitter and Instagram are such dumpster fires in different ways. People put their best selves forward on social media, and even if I know that logically, it still has the potential to make me really depressed. I could never delete social media or anything, because it has its upsides too, but I have to be very, very aware when it's a bad idea for me to scroll mindlessly through my feed. Sometimes I can't handle the portrayed perfection or the disheartening news or people being awful and combative. It's a small thing, but I don't keep Twitter or Instagram on my home screen on my phone anymore. Out of sight, out of mind."

—Julie, 19, Seattle, WA

Use Your Emotions for Good / Instead of trying to

ignore negative feelings when you have them, allow yourself to look at them differently and experience them with an understanding of their benefits. It can be hard—nothing is more aggravating than being told to look on the bright side when you're angry, afraid, or sad. But at the same time, anger fuels change and sparks motivation, fear protects you and challenges you to be bold, and sadness allows you to feel deeply. Use those things to your advantage.

Verbalize Your Needs / It's an extremely human thing to

feel frustrated when someone doesn't love us in the *right* way. We all
have unique love languages—ways we want to be shown appreciation,
fondness, and gratitude; things that make us feel seen and important
to our loved ones. But we also have our own personal ways of
showing love and appreciation, and how we give and want to receive
aren't always the same—which can lead to miscommunication and
misunderstanding between people who really, really care about each
other but show it in different ways.

So, you sometimes have to teach others how to love and care
for you—friends, family, and romantic partners. People aren't mind

readers! Without communicating to your best friend that, say, you get insecure about your friendship when you go for a while without seeing each other, she might keep thinking that you know she cares about you based on how often she makes sure to text even when she's busy. Or maybe it's about time to tell your partner that you'd take a quiet night in, cuddling and talking, over a bouquet of flowers any day.

Visualize / If you have trouble falling asleep at night, and even if you don't, a good alternative to counting sheep (boring) is to visualize positive parts of your day. Not only can it help you *not* to spiral out replaying the awkward or less-nice parts of your day (or, you know, a moment from a decade ago that FOR SOME REASON your gremlin brain loves to remind you about), but it's just plain pleasant and is another subtler way of practicing gratitude.

Volunteer / There's a lot of research that suggests doing things for others is great for mental health. And on top of that, it's wonderful medicine for loneliness, which is a really difficult emotion to self-soothe. You'll be around people, make connections, and have people thank you for your time and appreciate you for who you are.

Vulnerability / Allowing ourselves to be vulnerable is easier said than done, to say the least. There's no guidebook that teaches how exactly to let your guard down and offer yourself up to the terrifying possibility of being seen and known. But what you can do is look for small opportunities from day to day and challenge yourself to take them. Answer honestly when someone asks you how you are and you're not fine. Admit to a friend that something they said hurt your feelings. Ask for help. Teach people how to love you. It requires bravery, and opening yourself up to potential hurt and disappointment, but as Brené Brown writes in her book *Daring Greatly*, "Embracing our vulnerabilities is risky but not nearly as dangerous as giving up on love and belonging and joy—the experiences that make us the most vulnerable."

> **Embracing our vulnerabilities is risky but not nearly as dangerous as giving up on love and belonging and joy—the experiences that make us the most vulnerable.**
>
> **—Brené Brown**

Want / Things we think we *should* do have a habit of hanging over us like clouds: *I should work out more. I should be happier. I should be more grateful. I should have made more progress in therapy by now.* But the thing about *should* is that it often represents unrealistic standards, set by ourselves and others, and comes bearing judgment, guilt, and shame. When we focus on what we think we *should* be doing, we wind up ignoring or even forgetting what we *want*—not out of obligation, but out of passion.

Instead of *should*-ing yourself, try focusing on, *I want* and *I would like.* Think: changing "I should be a better friend" to "I want to be a better friend," or "I should eat healthier" to "I want to eat healthier."

You might find that reframing it makes it untrue. For example, if you've been telling yourself you should go to the gym more but can't honestly say you *want* to go to the gym more, maybe it's time to take the pressure off.

It might seem like a small tweak, but it's more motivational, shifting the focus away from the fear and judgment of ourselves that prevents us from being the people that we want to be.

Their Care: "Self-care is staying home on my day off even though I live in paradise and I 'should' be heading to the beach and getting a tan and a beer and meeting people. No! I want to rest. I want to spend time with my animals. Me time is therapeutic and I don't need to let anyone take that from me."

—**Anaurora, 29, Playa del Carmen, Mexico**

Weather / The weather can affect us in profound ways. Cold, dark days might leave you feeling tired and lethargic. Hot, swampy days might make you sluggish and cranky. A rainy night when you get to stay snuggled up inside might inspire peace and comfort. The perfect spring day might lighten your mood and make you all, "Um, wow, did this just cure my depression?"

Mood aside, the weather might also impact symptoms of a preexisting condition. One study found that 72 percent of rheumatology patients (such as those with arthritis or fibromyalgia) reported that low temperatures made their symptoms worse. Winter weather is also worse for a lot of people with asthma, since cold air is known to trigger asthma attacks *and* we tend to spend more time indoors, home to things like mold, pet dander, dust mites, and ash and smoke from fireplaces. If you deal with migraines, changes in barometric pressure could exacerbate symptoms. And that's just a few examples.

But, seriously, we can't control the weather, so what does this have to do with self-care? Awareness, for one. If you know which season is your bad season—whether that means a season you just hate or that impacts the way you function in some way—you can do a little bit of prep work to make it easier *and* you can resolve to go easier on yourself. Stock up on weather-appropriate clothes, get a sunlamp, make arrangements for accessibility (in case, say, you have a mobility issue that makes it's harder to run important errands when it's snowing), invest in a window AC unit, and get ready to double down on self-care routines you already know work for you.

SEASONAL AFFECTIVE DISORDER (SAD)

More than just the "winter blues," SAD is a subset of major depressive disorder. The difference between it and other types of depression is that it follows a seasonal pattern, meaning that the symptoms are present in certain months but completely absent in others. It actually doesn't have to do with the weather—it's a result of darker months and shorter days.

If you're not sure whether what you're experiencing is winter blues or something more serious, ask yourself, "How much are the symptoms I'm experiencing affecting my day-to-day life, my ability to perform at school or at work, or my important relationships?" Diagnosis or not, a doctor will be able to talk to you about treatment options, such as light therapy or antidepressants.

Weighted Blanket / If you've ever woken up on a cold morning trapped securely under a pile of warm blankets, you might get the appeal of being confined by a twenty-five-pound blanket. First introduced as a therapy tool, deep-pressure touch has turned into a popular answer for a lot of needs. People with anxiety, people with autism, and people who have trouble sleeping are only a few examples of the kinds of people who crave the sweet pseudo-coma provided by a weighted blanket. But let's be real: When the world sucks, the idea of being smothered by a really, really heavy blanket is pretty tempting for just about everyone.

Well /

Your "well" is a concept that mental health professional Kameelah Rashad shared with me, and much like self-care, it's different for everyone. Your well can be a place, person, or even activity or hobby—whatever it is, it's what you can return to time and time again to reap positive mental health benefits, whether that's feeling loved, relaxed, or safe, without the risk of diminishing return. It's your MVP of self-care.

Ask yourself, "Where do I go to feel nourished and affirmed? To feel understood?" Maybe it's a friend who always makes you laugh, someone who sends you loving texts, a conversation with your mom, being in nature, meditation, prayer, or even watching a video of your adorable baby cousin. Just make sure you know what your well is and that you go there often, using it as a chance to take a moment to breathe and gather your strength.

Win File /

We accrue so many tiny wins over the course of each day—little blips of happiness and pride in the form of sweet texts from friends, encouraging feedback from bosses, even the occasional genuine compliment on a dating app. On their own, they might not be the sorts of things you remember to reflect back on. But when you start to collect them in one place—a folder of screenshots, a Google doc, a running list in your journal—you can create a powerful resource to draw from when you need a boost.

Work–Life Balance / The boundaries between your work
life and your personal life might be blurry. After all, we live in a
burnout culture where we're inundated by messages of overworking,
monetizing our hobbies, and accruing side hustles. You can ease a
little of that pressure by making an effort to leave work on time, not
to check your email past a certain point at night, and in general, not
to think about your work responsibilities outside your office or work
space, and vice versa.

Of course, it's just as likely that your boss is the one smudging
the line between work and life, always expecting you to be on call
to answer emails or pushing you to stay late. That's a little harder to
rectify, but there *are* little ways you can firm up boundaries between
you and your boss, such as acknowledging after-hours requests with,
"Thanks for this! Will prioritize when I get in tomorrow," and see if
they catch on.

If you can't seem to balance the scales, no matter how hard you
try, it's worth considering whether your job is *really* right for you.
If your job is consistently driving you to burnout, unhappiness, and
exhaustion, don't hold out hope that it will get better—start looking
for a job that *won't* make you miserable.

Work / So often, when work comes up in the mental health
conversation, it's exactly in the context of the last entry—finding
ways to be happy and balanced *despite* the demands and pressures of
working. But for some people, throwing themselves into work brings
a sense of accomplishment, purpose, or distraction that is as healing as
acts of more traditional self-care.

As Anna North wrote for *The New York Times*, relaxing isn't
everyone's self-care: "Chilling out just doesn't work for me the
way work does. . . . Far better for me to put my mind to use. . . . I
remember finishing a daylong project in Iowa City last year, ahead of
the Iowa caucus, and realizing that all the worries that had entered
the city with me had been pushed aside by the voices of the people I
talked to, by the process of fitting them all together. To work, for me,
is to care for the self by putting the self aside." So if that sounds like
you, don't beat yourself up about it.

XXX / I probably don't need to tell you that masturbation and sex are great stress relievers. But if you need convincing, your brain rewards you for orgasming. When you get off, solo or with a partner or partners, you release oxytocin—which is a pretty damn blissful hormone—and afterward, your mind is chill, calm, kind of stoned, and everything feels freaking wonderful.

But you can also get a lot out of taking your time and masturbating ~mindfully~. It's a great way to get to know your body, get in touch with what turns you on, and TBH, just have a really, really great time pleasuring yourself. As a refresher, mindfulness is the practice of being present in the moment and being aware of your body, your feelings, and your individual senses. So, mindful masturbation is what it sounds like: embracing that level of focus and awareness while you're having sex with yourself. And while not every time you masturbate can be the picture of mindfulness (nor should it—we all have shit to do), you should definitely indulge in an occasional ritual of self-love.

WHAT DOES THAT LOOK LIKE?
HERE ARE SOME TIPS:

1. Throw the goal of orgasming out the window and just focus on exploration and pleasure.

2. Set the stage and create an ~ambiance~ to set the mood.

3. Pick a time when you know you won't be interrupted or distracted by the fear of being overheard.

4. Make sure to set out everything you need ahead of time (like lube, toys, etc.), and choose a variety so you can experiment.

5. If you need help quieting your thoughts so you can really focus, start with some nonsexual meditation or relaxation exercises like deep breathing.

6. Explore all your erogenous zones and how they respond to different types of touch.

7. When you're done—whether that's after you've had an orgasm or whenever you decide—take time to reflect on what you learned about your body.

Yes / Just like you should say no to more things you don't really want to do, you should say yes to the things that scare you but that deep down you want to try. Take that night class. Go to that party where you only know the host. Indulge your urge to take that solo vacation. More than that, though, you should say yes to the things you would normally avoid due to anxiety. This sounds awful, I know, but it's therapist-approved. While part of self-care is being mindful and avoiding triggers, a lot of the time where anxiety is concerned, avoidance only breeds more anxiety and can build up to the point of interfering with your life. If you never put yourself in a position to see that things will be OK, even if they're uncomfortable in the moment, you never give yourself the chance to learn to live with—and ultimately lessen—your anxiety.

Yoga / Like meditation, yoga is one of those things that either is or isn't your thing, but it can't hurt to try to see if its physical and mental benefits ring true for you. For yoga skeptics out there, it can really help to focus on the non-exercise benefits. I never thought I'd be a ~yoga person~ but after a back injury left me with months of chronic pain, I grew to appreciate yoga for its restorative benefits. For me, those were pain relief and recovery stretches. For you, it might be something different. Yoga can be what you make of it, and with a little research, you might find out that you connect with it more than you thought you would.

Their Care: "I'm a paraplegic, a cat dad, and a health nut, and I've put a lot of time and effort into becoming my best self because that's what the people around me deserve. My self-care takes the form of what a friend of mine calls self-constructive behavior. Every morning, I do yoga and meditate as soon as I wake up (and feed my cat). I think there's a lot to be said for starting the day by just being quiet with yourself. I have anxiety issues, so centering myself like this makes the rest of the day easier. Throughout the day, I sing, eat healthy, and play with my cat whenever a chance comes up. It's small stuff, but it keeps me going and feeling good, and that's what my self-care is all about—making it to tomorrow."

—David, 26, Portland, OR

Zzzz / It may be the only entry under Z, but sleep and mental well-being go so hand in hand they might as well be conjoined. Lack of sleep can seriously magnify feelings of unhappiness or depression and anxiety, just as a good night's sleep can provide you with the foundation you need to get through the day.

It's also common to get too much sleep, especially when you're depressed. And that actually works against you, since so much treatment for depression involves trying to live your life and be active. When you sleep too much, you feel groggy. There's a kind of threshold, like there is with food: You need it to be healthy, but too much of it is going to make you feel sick.

Your sleeping patterns can also give you clues about your health—specifically, things that might be wrong and that you can address to feel better! Many things cause insomnia, from stress to sleep disorders, and your doctor will best be able to help you figure out what's going on so you can get the sleep you need.

What Self-Care Do You Need

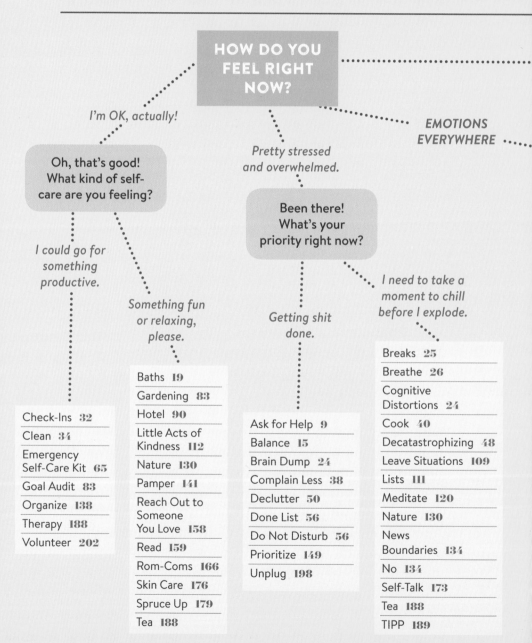

HOW DO YOU FEEL RIGHT NOW?

I'm OK, actually!

Oh, that's good! What kind of self-care are you feeling?

I could go for something productive.

Something fun or relaxing, please.

Pretty stressed and overwhelmed.

Been there! What's your priority right now?

Getting shit done.

I need to take a moment to chill before I explode.

EMOTIONS EVERYWHERE .....

Check-Ins 32
Clean 34
Emergency Self-Care Kit 65
Goal Audit 83
Organize 138
Therapy 188
Volunteer 202

Baths 19
Gardening 83
Hotel 90
Little Acts of Kindness 112
Nature 130
Pamper 141
Reach Out to Someone You Love 158
Read 159
Rom-Coms 166
Skin Care 176
Spruce Up 179
Tea 188

Ask for Help 9
Balance 15
Brain Dump 24
Complain Less 38
Declutter 50
Done List 56
Do Not Disturb 56
Prioritize 149
Unplug 198

Breaks 25
Breathe 26
Cognitive Distortions 24
Cook 40
Decatastrophizing 48
Leave Situations 109
Lists 111
Meditate 120
Nature 130
News Boundaries 134
No 134
Self-Talk 173
Tea 188
TIPP 189

Right Now?

Self-care may be specific to you and your needs, but in case you're feeling a little overwhelmed by all the info in this book or just want a quick answer, this chart will point you toward relevant entries that you may find helpful right in this moment.

Ugh, I'm sorry. How much effort do you think you can put in right now?

Like a pile of garbage, TBH.

Got it. Do you want a distraction?

A little bit, I guess.

As little as humanly possible. It's one of those days.

No, I can't concentrate on anything besides how angry/sad/overwhelmed I am.

YES, PLEASE.

Coloring Books 37
Cook 40
Dance 47
Drive 59
Joke 99
Little Acts of Kindness 112
Meditate 120
Move 124
Nature 130
Play 146
Puzzles 151
Rom-Coms 166
Therapy 188

ACCEPTS 4
Breathe 26
Burn Negative Thoughts 27
Cry 42
Feel Your Feelings 70
Journal 100
Let It Out 110
Name What's Upsetting You 129
Radical Acceptance 157
Self-Talk 173
Talk About Your Feelings 185
Therapy 188
TIPP 189
Understand Your Anger 195

Ask for Help 9
Bare Minimum 18
Ditch the Brave Face 53
Expecto Patronum 66
Fresh Clothes 76
Hydrate 90
Medication 120
Meet Yourself Where You're At 121
No 134
Self-Compassion 171
Self-Talk 173
Touch 191
Unplug 198

Baths 19
Change Your Environment 32
Eat 61
Games 81
Identify Problems 93
Indulge 94
Little Acts of Kindness 112
Lounge in Something Comfy 115
Make Your Bed 119
Move 124
Nature 130
Puzzles 151
Reach Out to Someone You Love 158
Read 159
Reward 165
Show Up 175
Splurge 177
Therapy 188

THERAPY FAQS

With input from Dr. Andrea Bonior and Dr. Ryan Howes

Q. HOW DO I FIND A THERAPIST?

A. Finding a therapist is kind of like dating. Seriously. Meaning it could take multiple tries before finding ~the one~ and at times the search might be frustrating. But ultimately, it will be worth it.

On a more practical note, there are two main avenues you can pursue to find a therapist:

1. **Go directly through your insurance.** Many insurance plans have helplines you can call or databases where you can search by location, method of therapy, and specialty.

2. **Search online.** My favorite place to search is the *Psychology Today* therapist finder because of its extensive filtering options. You can plug in your insurance or lack thereof, desired specialties, mental illness, and a ton of other specifications to find whatever you're looking for. Plus, you can find listings for mental health professionals in the United States, Canada, the United Kingdom, Australia, Austria, Belgium, Denmark, Ireland, Spain, Sweden, and Switzerland. Zocdoc is also a solid way to search, but it's not as customizable.

Referrals and word of mouth work, too. Your general practitioner might have a recommendation, and it never hurts to ask friends if they like their therapists and wouldn't mind your checking them out.

Q. THERE ARE SO MANY OPTIONS, THOUGH! HOW DO I PICK THE RIGHT THERAPIST?

A. You have to think about what you want in a therapeutic relationship—and there might be some trial and error. That's OK! Maybe you want a therapist who will challenge you and light a fire under your butt, or maybe you're looking for a space just to talk and process things with an unbiased third party. Maybe you want a therapist who reminds you of a mentor figure, or maybe you need a therapist who feels more like a peer and a friend.

On top of finding a therapist you feel comfortable with, it's helpful to find someone who is familiar with (or even specializes in) identities of yours or issues that are important to you. Some therapists will list those specialties in their bios, but always feel free to ask prospective therapists whether they feel equipped to talk about issues that pertain to your ethnicity, race, religion, gender, sexuality, politics, family situation, career, etc.

If you want help narrowing down your list of potential therapists before making an appointment, most will offer a free phone consultation with you ahead of time, which can give you a feel for how conversation flows and an opportunity to ask questions. It's not required, but it could save you some time and money if you get a bad feeling from someone you were prepared to make an appointment with.

Q. OK, OK, I GET IT, A STRONG MATCH IS MOST IMPORTANT. SO HOW—AND WHEN—DO I KNOW IF A THERAPIST IS A GOOD FIT FOR ME?

A. A good rule of thumb is to give it more than one session unless you get a distinctively bad feeling from a therapist and know it's not going to work out. The first session—often called intake—is typically structured and meant to get only the broad strokes of your history and concerns. It can be awkward and is not usually reflective of how therapy will actually go, so give yourself at least one or two more sessions to get a better sense of what it will *actually* be like.

Past that, it's kind of a gut feeling. Do you feel heard, understood, and respected? Can you see yourself opening up to this person and sharing the deep and difficult things in your life? Is there anything about the therapist that makes you keep your guard up when you're with them?

Q. WHAT DO THERAPISTS WRITE IN THEIR NOTES?!

A. Well, not all therapists take notes during session. But if they do, mostly likely they're jotting down notes to help them remember what you said during session so they can write their case notes after or refer back to important details in the future. They can be anything from "feels distant from friends but anxiety prevents her from reaching out" to "really into using astrology to explain her problems with dating."

Q. IS WHAT I SAY IN THERAPY REALLY CONFIDENTIAL?

A. According to the American Psychological Association (APA), what you say in therapy really does stay between you and your therapist, thanks to the Health Insurance Portability and Accountability Act (HIPAA), which dictates a national standard of privacy that protects patients' medical records and health information.

There are exceptions, though: A practitioner can share your information without your consent if they believe you pose a risk to yourself or others; if they're made aware of ongoing domestic violence, abuse, or neglect of children, the elderly, or people with disabilities; or if they receive a court order for it. But laws vary from state to state and each individual's situation is unique. If you're concerned about the implications of confiding in your therapist about these issues, look up your state's particular mandatory reporting laws. (By the way, all of this refers to the rights of adults. Confidentiality laws for minors vary more state by state.)

Q. HOW LONG DO I HAVE TO BE IN THERAPY?

A. It *really* depends. Unfortunately, there's no magic formula you can plug your neuroses into to find out how many sessions you'll need. But there are benchmarks you can look out for that might indicate it's time to move on.

If you went into therapy with a clear and specific goal in mind, then you ideally end your therapy when you meet your objective. You wanted to reduce social anxiety and now you can attend social gatherings without freaking out. You couldn't fly and now you can. And so on.

On the other hand, if you're in therapy for less concrete reasons—like, to get to know yourself better or to become your best self or to improve your marriage—it will have to be intuitive. You can keep going as long as you feel like you're growing and learning, which is something you can check in with your therapist about!

Q. HOW CAN I GET THE MOST OUT OF THERAPY?

A. Just going to therapy won't necessarily help—you have to participate. It takes collaboration, not just passively sitting back and waiting for results. Starting therapy prepared to do the work, both in and out of session, will go a long way.

Another helpful thing is to check in with your therapist about your progress. Do you still have the same goals you started therapy with? Do you both need to shake things up somehow?

Speaking up about the ways therapy isn't working for you is also an important part of the process. For example, maybe your therapist is dedicating too much session time to talking about your family and you don't feel like that's productive for you. Or maybe you want your therapist to push back against your bullshit more. A good therapist will listen to your concerns and correct course, within reason.

Q. ANYTHING ELSE I SHOULD KNOW?

A. Basically, THERAPY CAN BE FANTASTIC AND TRANSFORMATIVE. And if you're still not convinced, research shows that therapy—as long as you put in the work and find someone you trust and can rely on—is effective for the majority of people. So why not give it a chance?

MENTAL HEALTH RESOURCES

If you want to look after your mental health, sometimes self-care just isn't going to be enough. You might need to talk to someone or want to learn more about what you're going through, in which case, the resources below can be invaluable. Many of these resources are only in the United States, but many also provide international options on their websites.

CRISIS RESOURCES AVAILABLE 24-7:

The National Suicide Prevention Lifeline: If you're thinking about suicide or just need someone to talk to right now, you can get support by calling 1-800-273-TALK (8255).

Crisis Text Line: If you prefer to text rather than call, the Crisis Text Line is a great resource. Reach a trained volunteer by texting "HOME" to 741741.

The Trevor Project (thetrevorproject.org): TrevorLifeline and TrevorText provide LGBTQ+ crisis support that you can reach by calling 1-866-488-7386 or texting "START" to 678678.

The National Eating Disorders Association (nationaleatingdisorders.org): For crisis support and resources that can help, call NEDA's hotline at (800) 931-2237 or text "NEDA" to 741741 for crisis support.

The National Sexual Assault Telephone Hotline: If you need to talk to someone, call the 1-800-656-HOPE (4673) to talk to a trained professional from the Rape, Abuse & Incest National Network (RAINN) or visit rainn.org to chat over an instant messenger.

OTHER RESOURCES:

GoodRx (goodrx.com): If you take medication for whatever reason and find yourself in a sticky financial situation (or just like being thrifty!), GoodRx is a lifesaver. It compiles coupons for both brand and generic meds and tells you where you'll be able to find the cheapest option.

The National Alliance on Mental Illness (nami.org): Overall, NAMI is a great resource for finding treatment, symptoms of mental health conditions, treatment options, local support groups, education programs, helping family members get treatment, programs to find jobs, and legal issues related to mental health. They also have a helpline you can call with any questions: 1-800-950-NAMI (6264) or email info@nami.org.

National Sexual Violence Resource Center (nsvrc.org): If you or someone you love has been affected by sexual violence, check out the resources available from the NSVRC.

NeedyMeds (needymeds.org): This is another good option if you can't afford your medication or other health-care costs. It's a national nonprofit organization that offers free information on programs that will be able to help.

Psych Central (psychcentral.com/resources): This directory is probably the most extensive you'll find online. It's full of mental health resources, including general information, blogs, online communities, support groups, articles, quizzes, and books.

***Psychology Today* Therapist Finder (psychologytoday.com/us/therapists):** This, in my opinion, is the best place to start looking for a therapist. You can plug in your insurance or lack thereof, desired specialties, mental illness, and many other specifications to find whatever you're looking for. Plus, you can find listings for mental health professionals in the United States, Canada, the United Kingdom, Australia, Austria, Belgium, Denmark, Ireland, Spain, Sweden, and Switzerland.

PsyberGuide (psyberguide.org): There are a lot of apps out there that claim to help your mental health. Not only can you search PysberGuide for the best ones, you can also see expert reviews and ratings to pick one that's actually legit.

Substance Abuse and Mental Health Services Administration (samhsa.gov): If you or someone you love is struggling with an addiction, check out the resources available on the SAMHSA website or talk to a representative on their free, confidential national helpline by calling 1-800-662-HELP (4357).

FURTHER READING

When it comes to books related to mental health, there is such a huge variety, from personal memoirs to self-help books that can educate you, make you feel less alone, and support your efforts of self-care. I referenced some of the books below throughout this guide, but some are just genuinely lovely and helpful books I recommend for anyone looking to increase their understanding of all things mental health.

Are u ok? A Guide to Caring for Your Mental Health by **Kati Morton, LMFT**: A modern and relatable beginner's guide to mental health and mental illness.

The Art of Gathering: How We Meet and Why It Matters by **Priya Parker**: Self-care is social, and after reading this book, you'll never think of how you gather and connect with other people in the same way.

The Artist's Way: A Spiritual Path to Higher Creativity by **Julia Cameron**: Widely considered to be the seminal book on the subject of creativity, *The Artist's Way* also introduced me to the concept of morning pages—a daily journaling technique—that is a powerful self-care ritual.

The Collected Schizophrenias: Essays by **Esmé Weijun Wang**: Schizophrenia is still sensationalized and stigmatized as an illness, and Weijun Wang writes about her experience with schizoaffective disorder with courage and nuance.

Daring Greatly: How the Courage to Be Vulnerable Transforms the Way We Live, Love, Parent, and Lead by Brené Brown, PhD, LMSW: Mandatory reading for anyone who aspires to be a more vulnerable human.

Dot Journaling—A Practical Guide: How to Start and Keep the Planner, To-Do List, and Diary That'll Actually Help You Get Your Life Together by Rachel Wilkerson Miller: A super informative guide for anyone who wants to get into dot journaling—including for your mental health—but who might feel overwhelmed by all the information out there.

Emotional First Aid: Practical Strategies for Treating Failure, Rejection, Guilt, and Other Everyday Psychological Injuries by Guy Winch, PhD: My favorite self-help book that provides helpful advice for a ton of common mental health issues.

Everyone's a Aliebn When Ur a Aliebn Too: A Book by Jonny "Jomny" Sun: This picture book for adults might just make you cry and feel less alone in the world.

Expectation Hangover: Overcoming Disappointment in Work, Love, and Life by Christine Hassler: Managing expectations is easier said than done, but Hassler has it down to a science, and also offers tips for navigating disappointment.

The Four Tendencies: The Indispensable Personality Profiles That Reveal How to Make Your Life Better (and Other People's Lives Better, Too) by Gretchen Rubin: If you want to dive deeper into how you can motivate yourself and develop the habits discussed in this book, find out which of Rubin's "four types" you are.

The Friendship Fix: The Complete Guide to Choosing, Losing, and Keeping Up with Your Friends **by Andrea Bonior, PhD**: We don't think about the care and keeping of friendships the same way we do romantic ones . . . but we should. And this book is a great place to start.

Gmorning, Gnight! Little Pep Talks for Me & You **by Lin-Manuel Miranda (illustrated by Jonny Sun)**: An uplifting book by one of the greats, for anyone who needs help getting through the day.

How to Be Alone: If You Want To, and Even If You Don't **by Lane Moore**: A collection of vulnerable essays that will validate and soothe anyone who has ever felt lonely or isolated.

How to Be Single and Happy: Science-Based Strategies for Keeping Your Sanity While Looking for a Soul Mate **by Jennifer Taitz, PsyD, ABPP**: A compassionate guide to dating that doesn't condescend about the desire to be in the relationship and that acknowledges just how lonely singleness can be.

Hunger: A Memoir of (My) Body **by Roxane Gay**: Gay is one of the best voices out there when it comes to writing about food, weight, and self-image in a world that's determined to make us hate ourselves, and this memoir explores the line between self-comfort and self-care beautifully.

Insane Consequences: How the Mental Health Industry Fails the Mentally Ill **by DJ Jaffe**: A must-read for contextualizing self-care as privilege, and for anyone who wants to learn more about just how fucked up the mental health industry in the United States is.

Psychology: Essential Thinkers, Classic Theories, and How They Inform Your World by **Andrea Bonior, PhD**: Think of Bonior's book like an Intro to Psych class—but way more interesting and relevant to you personally.

Reading People: How Seeing the World Through the Lens of Personality Changes Everything by **Anne Bogel**: For all the personality quiz fans out there.

Reasons to Stay Alive by **Matt Haig**: Exactly what it sounds like, Haig's memoir will infuse you with hope and make you feel understood if you've ever battled with depression.

Sick: A Memoir by **Porochista Khakpour**: Khakpour writes with searing honesty about her illness that went undiagnosed for years, about racism and sexism in medicine, and about addiction, anxiety, and identity.

The Spirit Almanac: A Modern Guide to Ancient Self-Care by **Emma Loewe and Lindsay Kellner (illustrations by Charlotte Edey)**: A truly beautiful guide to self-care rituals through a historical and witchy lens. Worth it for the illustrations alone.

NOTES

Introduction

originally caught on as a medical concept: Easton, Kristen L. "Defining the Concept of Self-Care." *Rehabilitation Nursing*, vol. 18, no. 6 (1993): 384–87. ncbi.nlm.nih.gov/pubmed/7938895.

people who worked in "helping professions": Stamm, B. Hudnall. *Secondary Traumatic Stress: Self-Care Issues for Clinicians, Researchers, and Educators.* Lutherville, MD: Sidran Press, 1999.

self-care became political: Lorde, Audre. *A Burst of Light: And Other Essays.* Ithaca, NY: Ixia Press, 1988.

chronic loneliness: Holt-Lunstad, Julianne, Timothy B. Smith, Mark Baker, Tyler Harris, and David Stephenson. "Loneliness and Social Isolation as Risk Factors for Mortality." *Perspectives on Psychological Science*, vol. 10, no. 2 (2015): 227–37. journals.sagepub.com/doi/abs/10.1177/1745691614568352.

those with serious mental illnesses: National Alliance on Mental Illness. "Mental Health by the Numbers." nami.org/learn-more/mental-health-by-the-numbers.

most susceptible: Mental Health America. "Lesbian/Gay/Bisexual/Transgender Communities and Mental Health." July 14, 2016. mentalhealthamerica.net/lgbt-mental-health.

"Black & African American Communities and Mental Health." April 03, 2017. mentalhealthamerica.net/african-american-mental-health.

"Latino/Hispanic Communities and Mental Health." July 09, 2018. mentalhealthamerica.net/issues/latinohispanic-communities-and-mental-health.

"Native American Communities and Mental Health." June 30, 2016. mentalhealthamerica.net/issues/native-american-communities-and-mental-health.

A

ACCEPTS: Sunrise Residential Treatment Center. "DBT Tolerance Skills: Your 6-Skill Guide to Navigate Emotional Crises." September 13, 2017. sunrisertc.com/distress-tolerance-skills/.

dialectical behavioral therapy: *Understanding Mental Disorders: Your Guide to DSM-5.* Washington: American Psychiatric Association, 2015.

Emotional First Aid: Winch, Guy. *Emotional First Aid: Practical Strategies for Treating Failure, Rejection, Guilt, and Other Everyday Psychological Injuries.* New York: Hudson Street Press, 2013.

the science of neuroplasticity: Breuning, Loretta Graziano. *Habits of a Happy Brain: Retrain Your Brain to Boost Your Serotonin, Dopamine, Oxytocin, & Endorphin Levels.* Avon, MA: Adams Media, 2016.

half of people dealing with mental illness: National Institute of Mental Health. "Mental Illness." nimh.nih.gov/health/statistics/mental-illness.shtml.

B

catastrophic thinking: Sharf, Richard S. *Theories of Psychotherapy & Counseling: Concepts and Cases.* 5th ed. CA: Brooks/Cole, 2012.

boost your own serotonin: Breuning, Loretta Graziano. *Habits of a Happy Brain: Retrain Your Brain to Boost Your Serotonin, Dopamine, Oxytocin, & Endorphin Levels.* Avon, MA: Adams Media, 2016.

deep breathing is a powerful tool: Sood, Amit, and Mayo Clinic. *The Mayo Clinic Handbook for Happiness: A Four-Step Plan for Resilient Living.* Perseus Books Group, 2015.

summed it up best: Miller, Rachel Wilkerson, and Anna Borges. "Here's How To Use A Bullet Journal For Better Mental Health." BuzzFeed. August 19, 2016. buzzfeed.com/rachelwmiller/mental-health-bullet-journal.

C

naturally occurring compounds in the hemp plant: National Cancer Institute. "Cannabis and Cannabinoids." cancer.gov/about-cancer/treatment/cam/patient/cannabis-pdq.

"cognitive distortions": Burns, David D. *The Feeling Good Handbook.* New York, NY: Plume, 1990.

more susceptible to depression and anxiety: Ruscio, Ayelet Meron, Emily L. Gentes, Jason D. Jones, Lauren S. Hallion, Elizabeth S. Coleman, and Joel Swendsen. "Rumination Predicts Heightened Responding to Stressful Life Events in Major Depressive Disorder and Generalized Anxiety Disorder." *Journal of Abnormal Psychology,* vol. 124, no. 1 (2015): 17–26. ncbi.nlm.nih.gov/pmc/articles/PMC4332541/.

"The most regretful people on earth": Oliver, Mary. *Upstream: Selected Essays.* New York: Penguin Press, 2016.

actually releases endorphins: Orloff, Judith, MD. "The Health Benefits of Tears." *Psychology Today.* psychologytoday.com/us/blog/emotional-freedom/201007/the-health-benefits-tears.

The Crystal Bible: Hall, Judy. *The Crystal Bible 3.* Blue Ash, OH: Walking Stick Press, 2013.

D

decatastrophizing: Sharf, Richard S. *Theories of Psychotherapy & Counseling: Concepts and Cases.* 5th ed. CA: Brooks/Cole, 2012.

The Life-Changing Magic of Tidying Up: Kondo, Marie. *The Life-Changing Magic of Tidying up.* Ten Speed Press, 2014.

according to the American Dental Association: Mouth Healthy. "Your Top 9 Questions About Going to the Dentist—Answered!" mouthhealthy.org/en/dental-care-concerns/questions-about-going-to-the-dentist.

the American Optometric Association recommends: American Optometric Association. "Adult Vision: 19 to 40 Years of Age." aoa.org/patients-and-public/good-vision-throughout-life/adult-vision-19-to-40-years-of-age.

according to the American College of Obstetricians and Gynecologists: American College of Obstetricians and Gynecologists, Women's Health Care Physicians. "Frequently Asked Questions: Special Procedures." acog.org/Patients/FAQs/Cervical-Cancer-Screening#often.

creatures called Dementors: Rowling, J. K. *Harry Potter and the Prisoner of Azkaban.* Scholastic, 1999.

F

Fika: The Art of the Swedish Coffee Break: Brones, Anna, and Johanna Kindvall. *Fika: The Art of the Swedish Coffee Break, with Recipes for Pastries, Breads, and Other Treats.* Ten Speed Press, 2015.

sensory toys: Isbister, Katherine. "Fidget Toys Aren't Just Hype." *Scientific American.* May 18, 2017. scientificamerican.com/article/fidget-toys-arent-just-hype/.

G

feel measurably more content: Sood, Amit, and Mayo Clinic. *The Mayo Clinic Handbook for Happiness: A Four-Step Plan for Resilient Living.* Perseus Books Group, 2015.

H

The Four Tendencies: Rubin, Gretchen. *The Four Tendencies: The Indispensable Personality Profiles That Reveal How to Make Your Life Better (and Other People's Lives Better, Too).* New York: Harmony Books, 2017.

applying heat to an area improves circulation: "Self-care Approaches to Treating Pain." Mayo Clinic. July 26, 2016. mayoclinic.org/self-care-approaches-to-treating-pain/art-20208634.

The Little Book of Hygge: Wiking, Meik. *The Little Book of Hygge: Danish Secrets to Happy Living.* William Morrow, 2017.

I

—

technique to counteract negative thoughts: Sharf, Richard S. *Theories of Psychotherapy & Counseling: Concepts and Cases. 5th ed.* CA: Brooks/Cole, 2012.

imagery-based exposure: Cully, Jeffrey A., and Andra L. Teten, A. *A Therapist's Guide to Brief Cognitive Behavioral Therapy, 1st ed.* Houston: U.S. Department of Veterans Affairs, South Central Mental Illness Research, Education, and Clinical Center (MIRECC), 2008.

J

—

dark memes: Brown, Elizabeth Anne. "Suicide Memes Might Actually Be Therapeutic." *The Atlantic.* February 15, 2019. theatlantic.com/health/archive/2019/02/suicide-memes/582832/.

K

—

knitting dims the roar: Okun, Alanna. "Knitting Myself Back Together." BuzzFeed News. October 30, 2014. buzzfeednews.com/article/alannaokun/knitting-myself-back-together.

M

—

start by making your bed: McRaven, William H. *Make Your Bed: Little Things That Can Change Your Life . . . and Maybe the World.* Grand Central Publishing, 2017.

Expectation Hangover: Hassler, Christine. *Expectation Hangover: Overcoming Disappointment in Work, Love, and Life.* Novato, CA: New World Library, 2016.

P

—

Reading People: Bogel, Anne. *Reading People: How Seeing the World through the Lens of Personality Changes Everything.* Grand Rapids, MI: Baker Books, 2017.

Essentialism: McKeown, Greg. *Essentialism: The Disciplined Pursuit of Less.* Crown Business, 2014.

boost your mood: Lee, Min-Sun, Juyoung Lee, Bum-Jin Park, and Yoshifumi Miyazaki. "Interaction with Indoor Plants May Reduce Psychological and Physiological Stress by Suppressing Autonomic Nervous System Activity in Young Adults: A Randomized Crossover Study." *Journal of Physiological Anthropology,* vol. 34, no. 1 (2015). ncbi.nlm.nih.gov/pmc/articles/PMC4419447/.

aid in reducing anxiety: Kuratsune, H., N. Umigai, R. Takeno, Y. Kajimoto, and T. Nakano. "Effect of Crocetin from Gardenia Jasminoides Ellis on Sleep: A Pilot Study." Current Neurology and Neuroscience Reports. September 2010. ncbi.nlm.nih.gov/pubmed/20537515.

removing toxins: Wolverton, B. C., Anne Johnson, and Keith Bounds. "Interior Landscape Plants for Indoor Air Pollution Abatement." *NASA John C. Stennis Space Center*, September 1989. ntrs.nasa.gov/search.jsp?R=19930073077.

crassulacean acid metabolism: Heather Kropp, Angela Halasey. "Snacking on Sunlight." Arizona State University, *Ask A Biologist*. August 2, 2014. askabiologist.asu.edu/explore/snacking-sunlight.

Swedish fitness trend: Frymorgen, Tomasz. "Plogging is the latest Scandinavian lifestyle trend to rock your world." BBC. January 30, 2018. bbc.co.uk/bbcthree/article/237c63d4-0a54-406a-ae51-ad677a872456.

induce positive hormonal and behavioral changes: Carney, Dana R., Amy J. C. Cuddy, and Andy J. Yap. "Power Posing." *Psychological Science*, vol. 21, no. 10 (2010): 1363–368. doi:10.1177/0956797610383437.

using a pro-and-con list: Linehan, Marsha. *Cognitive-Behavioral Treatment of Borderline Personality Disorder*. New York: The Guilford Press, 1993.

problem you can solve: Miller, Rachel Wilkerson. "The Peace of a Puzzle." BuzzFeed. December 1, 2017. buzzfeed.com/rachelwmiller/the-peace-of-a-puzzle.

R

radical acceptance: Sunrise Residential Treatment Center. "DBT Distress Tolerance Skills: Your 6-Skill Guide to Navigate Emotional Crises." September 13, 2017. sunrisertc.com/distress-tolerance-skills/.

body scan meditation: Stanford Medicine, ELSPAP Mindfulness. "Body Scan Meditation." mindful.stanford.edu/additional-resources/self-care/body-scan-meditation/.

S

hurting yourself on purpose: National Alliance on Mental Illness (NAMI). "Self-Harm." nami.org/learn-more/mental-health-conditions/related-conditions/self-harm.

"psychological safety blanket": Tolentino, Jia. "The Year That Skin Care Became a Coping Mechanism." *The New Yorker*. December 18, 2017. newyorker.com/culture/cultural-comment/the-year-that-skin-care-became-a-coping-mechanism.

genuine smile: Kraft, Tara L., and Sarah D. Pressman. "Grin and Bear It." *Psychological Science*, vol. 23, no. 11 (2012): 1372–378. ncbi.nlm.nih.gov/pubmed/23012270.

twenty-five trillion miles away: NASA. "The Cosmic Distance Scale: The Nearest Star." imagine.gsfc.nasa.gov/features/cosmic/nearest_star_info.html.

T

said to have calming properties: Williams, Lawrence. E., and John. A. Bargh. "Experiencing Physical Warmth Promotes Interpersonal Warmth." *Science*, vol. 322, no. 5901 (2008): 606–07. ncbi.nlm.nih.gov/pmc/articles/PMC2737341/.

thanks to the Health Insurance Portability and Accountability Act: American Psychological Association. "Protecting Your Privacy: Understanding Confidentiality." apa.org/helpcenter/confidentiality.

TIPP: Sunrise Residential Treatment Center. Sunrise Residential Treatment Center. "DBT Tolerance Skills: Your 6-Skill Guide to Navigate Emotional Crises." September 13, 2017. sunrisertc.com/distress-tolerance-skills/.

controversial experiments: Harlow, Harry F. "Love in Infant Monkeys." *Scientific American*, vol. 200, no. 6 (1959): 68–74.

The Five Love Languages: Chapman, Gary. *The Five Love Languages: How to Express Heartfelt Commitment to Your Mate.* Nashville, TN: LifeWay Press, 2010.

U

actual physiological response to wanting food: Lindquist, K., and J. MacCormack. "Feeling Hangry? When Hunger Is Conceptualized as Emotion." *Emotion*, June 11, 2018.

"Anger is like a howling baby": Thich Nhat Hanh. *Anger: Wisdom for Cooling the Flames.* New York: Riverhead Books, 2002.

V

research that suggests: Jenkinson, Caroline E., Andy P. Dickens, Kerry Jones, Jo Thompson-Coon, Rod S. Taylor, Morwenna Rogers, Clare L. Bambra, Iain Lang, and Suzanne H. Richards. "Is Volunteering a Public Health Intervention? A Systematic Review and Meta-analysis of the Health and Survival of Volunteers." *BMC Public Health*, vol. 13, no. 1 (2013). bmcpublichealth.biomedcentral.com/articles/10.1186/1471-2458-13-773.

Daring Greatly: Brown, Brené. *Daring Greatly: How the Courage to Be Vulnerable Transforms the Way We Live, Love, Parent, and Lead.* London, England: Penguin Books, 2015.

W

72 percent of rheumatology patients: Ng, Jennifer, David Scott, Ashish Taneja, Peter Gow, and Ashmita Gosai. "Weather Changes and Pain in Rheumatology Patients." *APLAR Journal of Rheumatology*, vol. 7, no. 3 (2004): 204–06. onlinelibrary.wiley.com/doi/abs/10.1111/j.1479-8077.2004.00099.x.

worse for a lot of people with asthma: Metcalf, Eric. "Winter Asthma: Dealing With Asthma in Cold Weather." WebMD. webmd.com/asthma/features/winter-asthma#1.barometric pressure.

deep pressure touch: Krauss, K. E. "The Effects of Deep Pressure Touch on Anxiety." *American Journal of Occupational Therapy*, vol. 41, no. 6 (1987): 366–73. ncbi.nlm.nih.gov/pubmed/3688151.

people with autism: Edelson, Stephen M., Meredyth G. Edelson, David C. R. Kerr, and Temple Grandin. "Behavioral and Physiological Effects of Deep Pressure on Children With Autism: A Pilot Study Evaluating the Efficacy of Grandin's Hug Machine." *American Journal of Occupational Therapy*, vol. 53, no. 2 (1999): 145–52. designhub.it/cometa/wp-content/uploads/2017/09/The-American-Journal-of-occupational-theraphy.pdf.

"Chilling out just doesn't work for me": North, Anna. "Work Is My Self-Care." *The New York Times.* March 21, 2017. nytimes.com/2017/03/21/opinion/work-is-my-self-care.html.

X

you release oxytocin: Komisaruk, Barry R., Beverly Whipple, Sara Nasserzadeh, and Carlos Beyer-Flores. *The Orgasm Answer Guide.* Baltimore, MD: Johns Hopkins University Press, 2010.

Z

sleep and mental well-being: Sood, Amit, and Mayo Clinic. *The Mayo Clinic Handbook for Happiness: A Four-Step Plan for Resilient Living.* Perseus Books Group, 2015.

ACKNOWLEDGMENTS

The More or Less Definitive Guide to Self-Care literally would not exist without my editor, Batya Rosenblum, who saw potential in the BuzzFeed article that was the inspiration for this book, and my friend and editor, Rachel W. Miller, who tasked me with writing a guide to self-care for BuzzFeed in the first place. There is nothing cooler than a boss who supports your passion projects and someone looking at it and saying, "This could be a book!"

To my mom, who has been asking me, "So when are you writing your first book?" without fail for the last decade. To my sibling, Mars, who has been my partner in illness and queerness and shitty genes and someone I can always count on to understand. And to the rest of my family: Anthony, dad, the aunts, the uncles, and the cousins, Mama and Papa, and Grandpa Bob.

Thank you to Thrive Ops—or whatever our group chat will be called by the time this book comes out—for your inexhaustible enthusiasm and patience whenever I needed to rant and rave while working on this book. You all are the best cheerleaders and have been every step of the way. I couldn't ask for a more genuinely supportive and talented group, and I can't wait to line my bookshelves with your work.

To everyone whose existence in my life is a form of self-care: Anne, Ben, Jackie, Lottie, Hannah, Joey, Zac, Julian, Holden, Caitlin, Anjali, and the countless friendly faces on Mental Health Twitter who share their stories, check in, and heart my depression tweets in solidarity.

To the team at The Experiment, who made this book what it was: Matthew Lore, Beth Bugler, Zach Pace, Jennifer Hergenroeder, Ashley Yepsen, Anna Bliss, and Grace Rambo.

To the psychologists and therapists who have taken so much time over the years to answer this reporter's questions and from whom I've learned so much: Andrea Bonior, Ryan Howes, Jenny Taitz, Guy Winch, Kameelah Rashad, Eric Beeson, and many more. Thank you for the wisdom (and the free therapy)! And to the badass editors and bosses who have pushed me to be a stronger reporter and writer: Casey Gueren, Carolyn Kylstra, and Robert K. Elder.

Lastly—and I'm going to get cheesy here for a second—thank you to everyone who has ever reached out to me over the course of my career to share your story and your heart. Writing about mental health can be super draining, and every email, comment, tweet, and DM reminded me of the importance of talking about mental health and made me feel less alone. There aren't really words for how invaluable that has been to me.

ABOUT THE AUTHOR

 **ANNA BORGES** is a writer, podcast host, mental health advocate, and senior health editor for SELF. Previously, she was a senior health and wellness writer at BuzzFeed, where she helped build its mental health platform from the ground up. Her work has appeared in BuzzFeed, *Cosmopolitan*, The Outline, SELF, and more. She lives in Brooklyn with two cats, and you can find her making sure everyone in the group chat is practicing self-care. *The More or Less Definitive Guide to Self-Care* is her first book.